HAUNTED
FILES
FROM THE
EDGE

ABOUT THE AUTHOR

Philip J. Imbrogno has researched UFOs and other paranormal phenomena for more than thirty years and is recognized as an authority in the field. A retired science educator who taught earth science, astronomy, and chemistry for thirty-one years, he has been interviewed by the *New York Times* and *Coast to Coast AM*, has appeared on *The Today Show* and *The Oprah Winfrey Show*, and has been featured in documentaries on the History Channel, A&E, Lifetime, and HBO. Imbrogno worked closely with many top UFO investigators, including Dr. J. Allen Hynek and Budd Hopkins.

HAUNTED
FILES
FROM THE
EDGE

**A PARANORMAL
INVESTIGATOR'S
EXPLORATIONS INTO
INFAMOUS LEGENDS &
EXTRAORDINARY
MANIFESTATIONS**

PHILIP J. IMBROGNO

Llewellyn Publications
Woodbury, Minnesota

FIRST EDITION
First Printing, 2012

Cover design by Kevin R. Brown
Cover images: House: iStockphoto.com/Shaun Lowe
          Ghost: iStockphoto.com/Ivan Bliznetsov
          Window: iStockphoto.com/Shelly Perry
          Stairway: iStockphoto.com/Giorgio Fochesato
          Man: iStockphoto.com/Cameron Whitman
          Opened tomb: iStockphoto.com/Csaba Peterdi

Llewellyn Publications is a registered trademark of Llewellyn Worldwide Ltd.

Library of Congress Cataloging-in-Publication Data
Imbrogno, Philip J.
  Haunted files from the edge : a paranormal investigator's explorations into infamous legends & extraordinary manifestations / Philip J. Imbrogno. — 1st ed.
      p.   cm.
  Includes bibliographical references (p.   ) and index.
  ISBN 978-0-7387-2782-0
1. Parapsychology. 2. Supernatural. I. Title.
  BF1031.I44 2012
  130—dc23
                                                              2012009425

Llewellyn Worldwide Ltd. does not participate in, endorse, or have any authority or responsibility concerning private business transactions between our authors and the public.
  All mail addressed to the author is forwarded, but the publisher cannot, unless specifically instructed by the author, give out an address or phone number.
  Any Internet references contained in this work are current at publication time, but the publisher cannot guarantee that a specific location will continue to be maintained. Please refer to the publisher's website for links to authors' websites and other sources.

Llewellyn Publications
A Division of Llewellyn Worldwide Ltd.
2143 Wooddale Drive
Woodbury, MN 55125-2989
www.llewellyn.com

Printed in the United States of America

ALSO BY PHILIP J. IMBROGNO

*Files from the Edge: A Paranormal Investigator's Explorations
into High Strangeness*

*Ultraterrestrial Contact: A Paranormal Investigator's Explorations
into the Hidden Abduction Epidemic*

*Interdimensional Universe:
The New Science of UFOs, Paranormal Phenomena
& Otherdimensional Beings*

Night Siege: The Hudson Valley UFO Sightings

*Celtic Mysteries in New England:
Windows to Another Dimension in America's Northeast*

CONTENTS

Preface xi

Chapter 1: In the Shadow of Science 1

Chapter 2: Domestic Terror 11

Chapter 3: Angry and Friendly Spirits 35

Chapter 4: Ghosts of Sleepy Hollow 65

Chapter 5: The Curse of the Green Witch 81

Chapter 6: Extraordinary Manifestations 107

Chapter 7: Haunted Places 143

Chapter 8: Ghosts of the Alamo 161

Chapter 9: The Curse of Owlsbury 177

Chapter 10: Out of Time and Place 191

Chapter 11: Lands of Dreams and Visions 215

Chapter 12: The Unseen Universe 235

Further Reading 241

Bibliography 243

Index 249

PREFACE

The world of the paranormal is quite fascinating to explore, since it takes us outside of what we call normal everyday experiences. When dealing with the unknown, many people look upon it as an exciting adventure, much like the seafarers of the fifteenth and sixteenth centuries who sailed across the stormy Atlantic with hopes of making magnificent discoveries in strange new lands. The alien lands that existed beyond the Pillars of Hercules across the great ocean were very different from those explorers' home countries. They were full of wonders beyond the sailors' wildest dreams and were full of unimaginable dangers.

These brave explorers of long ago had a burning curiosity and an insatiable appetite for knowledge and new discoveries. This was the driving force that made them want to see what was over the next horizon.

In many ways, we who research and investigate paranormal events are like those great seafaring adventurers of old. The difference is we are not looking for new lands to discover, but a new reality that lies just beyond normal human perception.

IN THE BEGINNING

My interest in the paranormal began at a very early age. I paid many visits to my local library, reading books and magazines, and at home I watched all the television shows that dealt with the strange and unusual. Although I watched every type of paranormal presentation, my main interest was and still is the UFO phenomenon.

Who wouldn't be interested in such a topic? The thought of an alien intelligence visiting Planet Earth for scientific exploration in fantastic spaceships with exotic propulsion systems would inspire the imagination of any young person. Then one day my interest in hauntings and ghosts was triggered by one popular writer at the time by the name of Hans Holzer.

Born in 1920, Holzer was one of the most prolific and popular paranormal researchers and writers of the twentieth century. A member of both the American Society for Psychical Research and the British Society for Psychical Research, as well as the executive vice president of the Center for Paranormal Studies, in the late 1970s Holzer became research director of the New York Committee for the Investigation of Paranormal Occurrences.

He wrote hundreds of newspaper and magazine articles on psychic phenomena and related subjects. Through the 1970s he turned out numerous books on ghosts, the occult, and psychical topics that reached a popular audience. At his peak he wrote three to four books a year. Several of his books helped promote the spread of Wiccan and Pagan beliefs. In the early

1980s Holzer wrote two books about the so-called Amityville Horror: *The Secret of Amityville* and *The Amityville Curse*.

After reading several of his books and watching a number of television specials that focused on his investigations of "haunted places," I was intrigued. Holzer was, in my opinion, the first real ghost hunter, and although much of his work is criticized today, it was his passion that fueled my interest in this phenomenon. Today, as a result of his early explorations, I have become a more seasoned researcher. My ability as an investigator was enhanced, as I looked at the broader picture and not a small part of it.

Over the course of my thirty-plus years in this field, I have seen researchers (including yours truly) who were once wide-eyed weekend investigators probing the darkness with the hope of shedding some light on the focus of their passion evolve into seasoned investigators with professional backgrounds using their skills to explore and document a new frontier.

DOCUMENTING A HIDDEN REALITY

During my three-plus decades of investigating the paranormal, I have collected a great deal of data. For the most part, paranormal researchers do not actually investigate the paranormal directly; they study the reports of such events that have been experienced by other people.

Although I was fortunate enough to have witnessed a number of ghostly manifestations during my investigations, most of my work has been collected from the accounts of credible people who in my opinion experienced something truly incredible.

At the conclusion of each investigation, each individual case study was placed in a large binder and kept in my office, where they remained for years. At the time I really didn't know what to do with many of the more bizarre cases or how they applied to my main interest—the UFO phenomenon.

Although I collected a considerable number of paranormal reports made by excellent witnesses, I classified such cases as being "High in Strangeness."[1] In other words, these were experiences that were so bizarre that even true believers found them difficult to accept and impossible to explain. After cataloging and looking over the hundreds of High Strangeness case studies I had collected over the years, it was clear they had great diversity and spanned the entire paranormal spectrum. I feel it is important that the most well documented of these files be released to educate and inform the general public concerning experiences of a growing number of people who honestly believe they have had a brush with another reality.

In a previous book of mine, *Files from the Edge: A Paranormal Investigator's Exploration into High Strangeness*, I published a small percentage of cases from my files. The book included my investigations of experiences from individuals who claimed contact with strange beings, interaction with

---

1. *High Strangeness* is a term originated by the late Dr. J. Allen Hynek in 1973 to denote UFO cases that were so incredible they were difficult to accept. These include alien abductions, encounters with apparitions, strange creatures, and a variety of experiences that today are called paranormal.

unknown forces such as poltergeist activity, and sightings of creatures that definitely did not belong to our physical reality.

This work, *Haunted Files from the Edge*, is a continuation of cases from my private files. In this work, case studies are once again presented from reliable witnesses who had more than a brief encounter with the extraordinary.

Haunted Files from the Edge is different from its predecessor, since this work presents cases from my files that deal with hauntings in homes and geographical locations known for paranormal activity. When I say "haunted," I do not necessarily mean the sighting of a ghost. A haunted location— whether it is a human structure or a forest, valley, swamp, or mountain—refers to those areas in which frequent incidents of paranormal events are reported. These events could take the form of apparitions that are phantasmic in nature, monster-like creatures, poltergeists, and other forces that are not physically indigenous to the particular location in question.

The case-study categories are quite broad since the investigation of a so-called haunting can be very complex, and at times could present itself in a great variety of forms. Although some paranormal researchers have concluded that six types of hauntings exist, I believe there are only three.

The *first category* appears to be a "human" type of haunting. In this type of manifestation, the entity encountered seems to possess a human personality and emotions. These entities usually appear in full or partial human form. The entity frequently responds to changes in its environment and an attempt at contact from investigators or witnesses.

The *second category* is referred to as a "residual" type of haunting. In such a case, a scene from a past tragic event is replayed again and again and witnessed by a living person or persons.

The *third category* is the most frightening. In this type of haunting the entity seems to be intelligent, but not human. It is often hostile in nature. The physical manifestations that occur during this type of haunting can sometimes result in physical and psychological harm to the witness. Although most ghost hunters feel the entity responsible for this type of haunting is demonic in nature, I believe it may be the result of an interdimensional being. The reason why it behaves the way it does is unknown, and we can only speculate about its agenda.

Some of the case studies presented in this work involve so-called haunted homes, which can be classified in one of the categories above. In a number of accounts the paranormal experiences have evolved to such an uncontrollable degree that the people living in them had to move out. However, in some cases, after a lengthy investigation to identify the cause, I was able to resolve the problem one way or another. In most cases to the best of my knowledge these homes have remained quiet after the conclusion of my investigation. To me, this behavior indicates the presence of a living and thinking being that does not want to be identified—and not a mindless force.

In this work I also include my investigations that involve the appearance and disappearance of strange, apparently physical, human-like individuals that seem to belong to a different part of the space-time continuum. In other words, they are out of time and place and not part of our reality. Are they ghosts, aliens, or beings from another dimension accidently trapped here? Or are they explorers? These speculative theories will be explored later in the book.

SCIENCE AND THE PARANORMAL

I am a scientist, and I do believe paranormal experiences are real, or at least most of them. What makes me different from my colleagues is that I had an interest in UFOs, cryptozoology, poltergeists, and hauntings long before I became a science researcher and educator. I have attended schools that have a reputation for being skeptical about anything outside of mainstream science, yet despite those many years of education and mental conditioning, I remain open-minded.

During an investigation, my interest in science allows me to be objective, yet my interest in the paranormal gives me the advantage of approaching each case with non-prejudicial objectivity. During my early years of investigating strange happenings, the scientific part of me almost won out, and I became extremely skeptical of all claims of the paranormal. However, as the years passed and more cases came to my attention, it was apparent these people were experiencing something—but what? In the late 1970s I was finally able to merge my interest in the paranormal with my scientific training. At this point in my life both sides are no longer in conflict with each other, but actually work together in harmonious balance.

Most of the otherworldly experiences presented in this book are quite difficult for our modern society to accept as real. Yet in all the cases presented in this work I am convinced the witness is relating what they consider to be the truth, to the best of their recollection.

STANDING ON THE SHOULDERS OF GIANTS

In order for us to even partially understand the multitude of unknown forces in the multiverse, we must first know what questions to ask. No matter which avenue of research you follow, whether the study of the paranormal or a discipline accepted by modern mainstream science, any true and proven fact that forms the foundation of our knowledge was obtained from continuing the work of those who came before us. My knowledge of the paranormal is vast today only because I stand on the shoulders of giants. These great people from whom I built a foundation of knowledge include John Keel, John Fuller, Donald Keyhoe, Charles Fort, and Dr. J. Allen Hynek, just to mention a few.

Unfortunately, regarding the study of the paranormal, much of the next generation often refuses to learn from the success and failures of their predecessors. Perhaps this is one of the reasons we seem no closer to a solution than those pioneers who started it all almost one hundred years ago.

Paranormal investigators are slowly opening the door to another reality that borders our own. This other reality is a strange and exotic world into which few humans get a glimpse and most never see. One hopes that researchers will continue to gather new information to find the answers to the countless questions that have remained unanswered over the past five decades.

PHOTOGRAPHY: IS IT RELIABLE?

Many paranormal investigations are not conducted in a home or other structure, but outdoors. Photography offers a good record of what the location was like. In the old days we had to wait for our developed prints to be mailed back from the photo lab. There was always a hope the pictures might have imaged some type of paranormal event.

During the mid-1970s and early 1980s I set up my own darkroom and was able to process color and black-and-white film to my specifications. I was also able to develop color slide film, which was a preference at the time since the resolution was much better. This was an important tool in my investigations, since photographic data and evidence could be obtained within twenty-four hours.

Today we have digital photography, and images can be uploaded into a computer instantly. Digital is very different from film, since it uses pixels to record an image rather than silver compounds. As a result, there are a greater number of people taking photographs, in part because we no longer have to pay to develop them, which, if you took enough photos, used to be very expensive.

One of the problems with digital photography, however, is that when used in conjunction with programs like Photoshop, images of ghosts and UFOs can be easily faked. The Internet is full of alleged paranormal pictures. It is my opinion that the majority of them are not authentic. If film is used, then the negatives can be studied in detail. Microscopic examination of color and black-and-white negatives, or positive transparencies, can immediately rule out a hoax.

Over the years I have collected images that, in my opinion, are real, because the original positive transparency film and negatives were obtained for an in-depth analysis. When people send me supposedly paranormal images by e-mail taken with a digital camera, I am very cautious to give my seal of approval. Unless I am able to talk with the witness face to face over several interviews and visit the site where the experience took place, it is doubtful any digital photographic evidence can be verified without a shadow of doubt.

PARANORMAL FILING SYSTEM

To date I have accumulated 893 personally investigated case studies. Also, there are another 954 that I have not personally looked into, since most of them were e-mails or letters that detail an experience. Sometimes the witness does not want to go any further than a letter describing an experience. In many of these cases that come to my attention via e-mail, the name is left out and replaced by a handle. It appears people are still reluctant to have their name associated with an encounter with the paranormal.

My filing system is simple. First of all I identify each case by the type of occurrence. For example, encounters with an unknown aerial object are classified as *UFOs*, while ghost sightings are placed in the category of *apparitions*. Poltergeists, electromagnetic phenomena, are classified as a *paranormal force*, while the sightings of creatures such as sea serpents,

Bigfoot, and alien-like creatures are placed in the *creature* category. People who claim alien abduction or channeling are placed in a special file labeled *CONTACT*.

Next, each case is given a code that describes if it was personally investigated by me or the result of a letter, e-mail, or phone interview. Also, another code is added that pertains to whether or not the case contains photographic or other types of documentation.

Finally, a reality probability rating is given, with 0 being incomplete and 5 the highest probability of the experience being real and related exactly as it happened. Probability is the most important part of the filing system, since these cases are personally investigated by me and resulted in an investigation that may have taken days, weeks, or months to complete. Out of 893 cases, the probability breakdown is as follows:

Probability Rating	Number of Cases
0	77
1	53
2	91
3	247
4	232
5	193

It is clear from the numbers above that I will only look into a case and do a detailed study if it has promise. In my earlier years a considerable amount of my time was spent organizing the files and making sure all the data was protected and secure. As I get older it is becoming more of a chore, and I will often place information in a "holding" notebook and not follow up on the material. Recently, I have been trying to digitize as much information as possible since a good number of the transcripts are twenty or more years old and starting to fade and discolor. The first priority was to get drawings, photographs, and other data that can be reproduced stored in my computer. To date I have used over 400 gigabytes of information and had to upgrade with an external drive that is several terabytes in size.

PARANORMAL CERTIFICATION

Over the past five years there has been a great interest in the paranormal. If you engage in a conversation long enough with someone, chances are that person will tell you about a paranormal experience they had or that someone they know had. This interest has led to a considerable number of people wanting to find out more. To satisfy their curiosity these people start looking for groups to join. In many cases they hope to become paranormal investigators and join the excitement in a field that is still in its infancy. These people become true believers. They want to believe that there are forces out there that defy explanation. Most will not accept any conventional cause for an alleged paranormal occurrence, even if it is obvious that something strange did not take place. They back people who are perpetrating a hoax—not for personal gain, but only because they want to believe too much.

To many of these weekend investigators, the paranormal is a game they play to amuse themselves when there is nothing else to do. Whether they believe or not, what they are investigating is not important to them, since it's fun—until of course they have an experience themselves. If a person is very active in the field, sooner or later they will witness a paranormal event. When this takes place the investigation is no longer a game, but a reality. At this point most are frightened away and drop their interest in the paranormal and take up kite flying or another harmless hobby.

Ever since the emergence of paranormal reality television shows, paranormal and ghost-hunting groups have sprung up all over the country. These groups have prospective members go through a testing phase before "certifying" them as paranormal investigators, UFO investigators, or ghost hunters. After the prospective member passes all the written tests and field examinations, they slap their hard-earned money in the palm of the group's president. The new "graduate" is awarded a card that identifies them as a ghost hunter, UFO investigator, and so on. Proud of their newfound status, these people start displaying their ID cards to witnesses and sometimes the authorities, who for the most part are not impressed!

I find this idea of having people go through a paranormal certification program quite amusing and sometimes just plain old annoying. The majority of these so-called certified card-carrying paranormal investigators should not be in the field at all! Also, in some cases I have found the training of ghost hunters, UFO investigators, and even Bigfoot hunters is nothing more than a smart con person's way of making an extra buck.

If you are serious about investigating one or all aspects of the paranormal, you don't need classes or to become "certified," and you certainly don't need a membership identification card. All that is required is a curiosity and a true desire to make known what is unknown.

The best way to break into this area of research is to work side by side with someone who is experienced and published in the field. The study of the paranormal today is much like astronomy was back in the fourteenth century. During that time there were a lot of wild ideas, wide-eyed speculation, mysticism, and, yes, even con men, but out of this confusion and craziness a true science was born.

History has a tendency to repeat itself. Perhaps several hundred years from now historians will look back at the twentieth and twenty-first centuries as a time when a new science was born. One hopes they will remember this century in which we now live as a point in history when the human species took its first baby steps into a new reality.

The next twelve chapters will take you on a trip to a realm that has been part of my life for the last three decades—a place you thought only existed in your dreams or perhaps your nightmares. Welcome to my world!

CHAPTER 1

IN THE SHADOW
OF SCIENCE

Although I was a science educator for over thirty years, I, unlike many of my colleagues, have an open mind when dealing with the so-called borderline or fringe sciences. Much like Batman, I lived a dual life: by day a mild-mannered science teacher, and at night and on weekends a paranormal researcher who goes out on exciting adventures to explore unknown worlds and track down strange creatures and otherworldly forces.

Many of my former students and their parents know about my involvement in studying strange phenomena. I was frequently asked questions by students that were outside our normal classroom discussion. The most common ones are "Are there aliens?" "Are you an alien?" and "Do you think there are such things as ghosts?"

Former students also ask me if their house is haunted because they hear noises during the night. Of course I skillfully maneuver around the questions and tell the younger children the things they hear that go bump in the night are nothing more than their house settling, or hot and cold water pipes expanding and contracting.

However, I believe that some claims of paranormal events are very real. I spend most of my weekends and vacation time trekking across the northeastern United States, and sometimes other parts of the country, tracking down clues to help me find out more about this other reality that has been mistakenly labeled as being supernatural in origin. (What we call the "supernatural" could be science we do not yet understand.) Although I have slowed down over the years, younger and less-experienced researchers still have trouble keeping up with me.

HEAR, SEE, SPEAK NO PARANORMAL

During the past three decades I have finely tuned my investigative skills. I have also acquired an arsenal of instruments to aid me in my quest to document what many scientists believe is not documentable.

On many occasions I proved my esteemed colleagues wrong and showed them images and data that verify there is an unseen world around us. The response from these esteemed men and women of science is usually the same. They look at the data and say something like "Mmm, interesting"—then walk away. It's almost as if they are afraid to admit to themselves that what they are seeing is real and unexplainable.

My opinion is that in some incidents this denial is the result of fear, a fear that makes them reject the idea that there are forces in the multiverse of which we humans have no knowledge and, most frightful of all, no control over.

The best example I can give took place about twenty years ago, when an amateur astronomer in Connecticut saw something strange while observing the moon. Through his telescope he noticed a bright ball of light slowly moving across the lunar surface.[2] This avid stargazer was quite experienced and knew this was strange, so he quickly hooked up his camera to the telescope and began taking photographs using color slide film. Although the final images were a little blurry, the lunar craters could be seen and the light was a clearly defined sphere, light yellow in color.

This was not some strange light reflection caused by the bright moon or misaligned optics. The object was actually illuminating the ground below as it moved across the lunar surface. The sphere of light then hovered above a large crater and projected a light that illuminated the dark crater floor. The next frames show two bright bursts of greenish light ejecting from each side of the object as it blasted off the lunar surface into space. After it did this, in a flash the object was gone!

I showed the sequence of ten pictures separately to two astronomers who specialize in observing the moon. As if

---

2. The amateur astronomer was using a Schmidt-Cassegrain telescope with an eight-inch mirror at 150 power.

reading a script, both took a quick look and said, "I'm busy right now and really can't give you my opinion of this at the moment." I did notice by the expressions on their faces that both of them found the images perplexing, but they refused to show interest or make an educated comment.

My interest in UFOs always precedes me in scientific circles. Since my ideas are considered "radical" by most scientists, several people who are not secure at their jobs often avoid me like Typhoid Mary. As soon as the astronomers considered the series of photographs to be paranormal or UFO-related, both wanted to stay clear. After all, a professional astronomer does not want to be quoted as saying the lights represented something moving across the lunar surface that can't be explained—in other words, a UFO! Although the photographs were taken in the 1980s, today they remain one of the best pieces of photographic evidence of *transient lunar phenomena,* or TLP.

TLP simply refers to short-lived lights, colors, or other changes in appearance of the lunar surface. The strange lights are sometimes stationary on the floor of a dark crater, or they can be seen moving slowly or quickly across the surface of the moon. Almost 90 percent of all sightings are made using a telescope by amateur astronomers.

Sightings of TLP go back to the early eighteenth century, with some events being observed independently by multiple witnesses. Sir William Herschel, who is credited with discovering the planet Uranus, reported that he saw strange lunar lights on numerous occasions in 1787.

The majority of transient lunar phenomena is documented in written reports and not photographed. Because of this, it is extremely difficult to do a comparative qualitative analysis on the phenomenon. Most modern reports concerning TLP are never published in scientific journals because of the increased public interest in UFOs. As a result of this, the lunar scientific community rarely discusses these observations among themselves and will often evade answering questions about TLP asked by members of the media.

It's apparent that the majority of established people in the scientific community will not get involved with anything that even has a slight hint of the paranormal attached to it. TLP may be a natural lunar phenomenon, but we will not find out the truth until mainstream astronomy initiates their thinking with an open mind.

Over the years I have accumulated a great number of drawings, diagrams, taped sounds, and photographic images using both the old type of emulsion film and the more modern digital. Most of this material is vague and the images are blurry. Perhaps someday analytical technology will improve, and these images can be enhanced to crystal clarity. On the other hand, over the years I have also been able to obtain a number of clear images of UFOs and various other phenomena taken by reliable people.

For reasons unknown to me, most paranormal researchers and the general public believe blurry photographs of UFOs and other types of paranormal phenomena are more likely to be real rather than something clear and well defined. When you show someone a nice, sharp image of a

UFO, apparition, or some strange creature like Bigfoot, the response is always the same: "This can't be real!" I always ask, "Why not?" and get no reply.

Whenever I am approached by someone who claims that they had contact with beings from another reality—whether angels, devils, or extraterrestrials—a red flag goes up. Most of these people who claim to channel information from a "higher source" believe they were specially selected for this purpose. The information is channeled through the individual and usually takes the form of automatic writing, music, verbal teachings, and sometimes detailed drawings and illustrations. Of the 201 cases in my files, only twelve have convinced me the individual is or was in contact with something other than their own imagination.

The best example of what I believe is a true case of contact of this nature involves a night watchman who claimed an angelic extraterrestrial channeled technical drawings through him. The drawings he produced are in vivid color and of devices that are beyond our technology. However, as with all cases of this type, only enough information is given to get our interest.

When the late Dr. J. Allen Hynek showed a number of the diagrams to scientists at several major universities, they were amazed by them and wanted to talk to the individual who produced them. When these learned professors of science were told how the drawings were produced, however, they displayed the same predictable behavior and walked away laughing under their breath.

Another example of this negative attitude of the scientific community to accept new and radical ideas concerns a geological oddity called the Balanced Rock in North Salem, New York. The rock is approximately sixty tons of granite perfectly balanced on six crystalline limestone rocks that have been carved in a conical shape. The Balanced Rock has been the scene of a great number of paranormal events, including UFO sightings, alien abductions, and the appearance of hooded apparitions. Also, and more frequently, people living in the area have reported unusual balls of multicolored lights circling around the Balanced Rock at low altitude. The very sight of this object gives one the impression that it was placed on the pedestal stones by intelligent beings with a purpose and is not a freak of nature.

The Balanced Rock is a popular attraction for the town of North Salem and is now considered a landmark in New York State. If you ask a geologist about the stone, he or she will most likely say that it is nothing more than a glacial erratic pushed down from Canada by giant sheets of moving glaciers during the last ice age eighteen thousand years ago. However, many other open-minded researchers, including myself, believe that the stone was placed there more recently, perhaps three or four thousand years ago, by human beings.

The Balanced Rock looks exactly like a ceremonial table stone called a *dolmen*. These megalithic structures are found in the British Isles and were used several thousand years ago as a marker to denote a special event or burial of an important person.

A new theory that is gaining acceptance by historians of New York is that the giant rock was placed there by European explorers centuries before Columbus sailed to the "New World." Just how these ancient people lifted and perfectly placed the sixty tons of granite on the pedestal stones is unknown.

Twenty years ago I asked a well-known geologist from Yale University what he thought of the Balanced Rock. His reply was a quick "Nothing more than a glacial erratic left over from the last ice age." When asked if he ever studied it in person, the answer he gave was a quick "no."

This seemed strange to me. How could someone who claims to be a scientist, the top in his field, come to this conclusion when he had never seen the artifact or researched it for himself? As a matter of fact, there has been no detailed research done on the Balanced Rock from any major university or college in New York or New England. Independent researchers like me have spent many hundreds of hours studying the Balanced Rock and have come to the conclusion that it is not a natural formation.

Over the years I published several articles concerning the North Salem artifact that appeared in a number of publications, including the New York *Daily News*. The articles presented evidence that the Balanced Rock was placed there by ancient European explorers as a marker and is not a freak act of nature.

In 2009 the town of North Salem took down the old sign near the Balanced Rock, which had simply said "A glacial erratic," and replaced it with one that indicates it is a dolmen or ceremonial stone possibly placed there by Druid and Celtic explorers centuries before Columbus.

The only reason why mainstream science has shied away from mysteries like the two I've mentioned in this chapter is because they have paranormal events attached to them. This attitude has to change if we are ever to find answers to the many mysteries on our small planet. Once the evidence of something incredible is connected to the paranormal, no matter how interesting, it may be that the majority of the scientific community turns a deaf ear to it. Like the proverbial three monkeys, these scientists choose not to hear, see, or speak a word of the paranormal.

CHAPTER 2

DOMESTIC TERROR

When a paranormal event takes place in the home it is difficult to deal with, especially if children are involved. I investigated the following case in the early summer and fall of 1981, and it involves a family who moved into an old colonial house in Connecticut. The disturbances in the home began as soon as they moved in. After a month of paranormal experiences, the family could not take any more and contacted me for help.

This case represents one of many incidents in which a malevolent force created so much terror that the family had to vacate their home. Although the story that follows may sound like the plot for a Hollywood horror movie, it was a real experience. This was one of the most well-documented and convincing cases of a haunting I have ever investigated in all my years of researching the paranormal. It is my opinion, and that of all those who entered this "cursed" house, that it was truly haunted and a place where an unseen reality crossed and clashed with our own.

THE CURSED LAND

An opportunity to move to a small town in the country was quite exciting to a family of five who had lived in the city all their lives. It was a miracle they were able to find a three-bedroom house in a prestigious Connecticut town that had a low crime rate and was only a forty-five-minute drive from New York City. This was an opportunity the family could not turn down, since the rent was only 150 dollars per month.

The children were three healthy, active boys—ages five, seven, and ten—who were raised in an inner-city environment. At first the eldest son was not happy at the thought of leaving his friends and starting at a new school. However, the boy changed his mind quickly and got very excited about the move when his parents told him the new house had a large front and back yard. When the parents told all three boys they might be able to get a dog, they all cheered loudly.

To the skeptical young father the home sounded like too good of a deal. He wondered why it was vacant, especially since it was a time when many couples were looking for a quiet and safe place to raise their children.[3] He called the

---

3. The time was 1981. Quite a few people, especially families from New York City, were flocking to the suburbs of New York and coastal Connecticut looking for housing.

landlord and arranged a tour of their prospective new home for the following Saturday in the early afternoon.

That Saturday they all drove to Connecticut, and the children were very excited since this trip was an adventure into another state, a place that they had never been. However, this was to be the beginning of an almost two-year-long journey into the darkest realms of the paranormal.

They were met at the house by the landlord. The young couple could not believe what they saw: the property was beautiful, with lush bushes and beautiful flowers.

They entered the house and were delighted to see two real fireplaces and a floor made up of thick pine planks. The owner explained that the floor was original and that the house had been built in the late 1700s. The house was in great condition for its age, and the rooms were large and airy.

The young husband became very curious and asked why the place hadn't already been taken for such a low rent. The landlord explained that a good number of people had lived in the house over the last five years, but they moved out or he asked them to leave because they didn't take care of the house or property.

The youngest son then began to breathe heavily and ran out of the house to the front lawn, screaming that a "man" wanted to hurt him. His parents ran after him and the landlord followed, muttering faintly, "Oh no, not again." The couple and the other two young boys asked the child what was wrong. He said, "I heard the voice of a man say if we stay in the house we are all going to die."

The couple thought he was scared about being in a new place. They calmed the boy down by telling him it was just wind coming through the fireplace. The couple apologized to the landlord and explained the children had lived in an apartment complex all their life with plenty of people around, and this was the first real home they had been in. They also thought it was because the property was very isolated. That, combined with the thought of leaving his friends, may have spooked him.

The parents and landlord finally coaxed the child to go back into the house, and they continued the tour with the two bedrooms upstairs. They all walked up the steep staircase that led to two large bedrooms on the top floor. The stairs were so steep that the couple feared someone, especially the children, might fall down during the night. This was a major concern since if someone tripped, they would certainly fall all the way down without stopping.

The first bedroom was large with slanted ceilings, which was a popular design in eighteenth-century construction. As they walked through the doorway that led into the second bedroom, there was an unexplained chill. They asked why it was so cold, especially on a July day. It was a chill that crept deep in the bones and made the hair on the back of their necks stand up. The wife said, "This is creepy. Why is it so cold?"

The landlord replied that it happened sometimes, and no one could figure it out. He thought it had something to do with the closet connecting to the cellar by a "hidden" passage.

"You mean there's a secret passage in the closet?" the wife asked. The landlord replied that the tunnel was constructed in the early nineteenth century, and the rumors were it had something to do with the Underground Railroad, but he wasn't sure.

One thing *was* for certain: the room had an unnatural feeling to it. The children stood outside the door, and when asked to join their parents they refused to come in, stating that "it felt creepy." The landlord then tried to lighten up the situation and said, "Well, in the summer you'll save on the electric bill, since you won't need an air conditioner in here."

Despite the strange feeling the entire family had, they still decided to take the house. The deal was too good to pass up, and finally the children would be in a safe neighborhood with good schools.

The couple asked the landlord if they could have a dog, since the children had always wanted one. His reply was that if they said yes to the deal that day and moved in by the end of the month, they could have as many pets as they liked. When the children heard they could get a dog for sure, the unsettled feelings they'd had about the house were replaced by joy and loud cheering. The family all agreed that they wanted to live there, and a lease was signed for two years. Over the next several days they slowly began moving boxes into the house, saving the heavy furniture for last.

On the last day of moving into the house, the husband unlocked the front door to begin the tedious task of moving in the furniture. As he entered the front door with his wife, the friends and relatives standing behind him all were shocked at what awaited them. The boxes were all open and many of them were turned over. Also, several dishes had been taken out of the kitchen box, and it looked like they had been shattered by some force that had thrown them at the wall and floor. The feeling was that somebody or something definitely did not want them there.

At first they feared that someone had broken in and gone through their belongings, but nothing was missing. The doors and windows were locked, and there was no evidence anywhere of a forced entry. The aunt of the wife remarked how strange it was and then asked the location of the bathroom. After being directed there, she closed the door and within minutes began to scream. She ran out of the bathroom, hysterically crying and saying that while washing her hands she saw a "horrible face of a man" in the mirror with slashes all over his face. When she turned around, there was no one there and the image was gone. From that day on, this aunt would refuse to come back to the house even for special occasions.

By the end of the week the family was completely moved in with their new dog, a mixed English spaniel, and ready to spend the night. The oldest boy took the bedroom downstairs, while the two youngest would share the room adjoining the master bedroom, where their parents would sleep.

That evening they invited a friend of the father to stay for dinner. The entire family and the friend sat around the table enjoying their meal when the friend, who had a clear view of the front door, said, "Hello, who are you?" His face then went pale, and while trying to speak, he kept stuttering.

The couple asked him what was wrong. He told them, "There was a man standing by the front door. He was dressed in clothes that looked like the early 1800s. He tipped his hat and smiled at me and vanished in a puff of fog." At first they thought he was fooling around but soon realized their friend was dead serious about what he had seen. They played the event down so the children would not get scared, since the house being haunted was brought up more than once during discussions among relatives and local neighbors who dropped by to say hello.

It was getting late, and the mother sent the boys to bed. The oldest son was a little scared to sleep alone so he brought the dog into the room with him. He climbed into bed and, despite thoughts of ghosts and monsters, fell asleep quickly.

At about two o'clock in the morning, he woke up to the sound of the dog growling. He looked to the head of the bed and saw the dark outline of a "tall man" who had a glow surrounding the top of his head. The dog was staring right at the man, growling. The boy then pulled the covers over his head and began screaming. His parents and brothers ran down the stairs and turned on the lights. They asked him what was going on. The boy told them what he saw, and the parents tried to convince him it was a dream. They sat with him for about an hour until he once again drifted off to sleep.

Early in the morning, the young wife got out of bed after a restless sleep. She told me during our first interview: "That first night I felt that someone was in the dark corner of the room near the closet that led to the secret passage. I could feel her eyes staring at me. I say *her*, because the presence felt female in nature and very angry. I don't understand how I knew this; it was just a feeling. I got up out of bed and checked on the two young ones in the next room; they were sleeping quietly. I then began to walk down the stairs and heard a voice in my right ear whisper, '*Get out of my house or you will die.*' I felt two hands on my back push me with great force, and I fell down the stairs all the way to the bottom. The crashing sound of me falling woke up everyone in the house, and they all came running to find me unconscious."

Although she had a slight concussion and fractured her right arm, the injuries were not serious. However, the doctors told her she was lucky she didn't break her neck or back. Later, a few days after her visit to the emergency room, the wife told her husband about the voice she'd heard. She felt that the woman who was in the bedroom at night was the same one that pushed her down the stairs. It was clear to the couple that something in the house wanted them out. They also began to understand why the rent was so cheap and why no one had lived in the house for any length of time.

That evening, as they all were in the living room watching TV, the dog began to act very restless and started crying. A noise came from upstairs; it sounded as if someone wearing heels was walking back and forth on the wood floor in the parents' bedroom. The dog ran to the stairs and began barking, but he would not climb higher than the bottom landing. It sounded like a real person was upstairs; they thought perhaps someone had climbed up on the roof and through the window.

Then without warning there was a loud series of bangs on the floor, as if someone was jumping up and down. The husband ran to the stairs and started climbing them. He reached for the light, but none of the lights upstairs would go on. He went to the kitchen, got a flashlight, and cautiously made his way up the stairs into the bedroom. Nothing was seen in the first bedroom. As he entered the rear bedroom, out of nowhere a blast of "ice-cold" air moved passed him and sent shivers up and down his spine.

He told me during an interview, "It felt like death, and there was a presence that scared the hell out of me, something evil." He tried the switch again, and to his relief the lights went on. His family was at the base of the stairs calling to him and trying to find out if he was all right. He replied that he was, and there was nothing out of place in either bedroom.

After calming the children down, they went back to watch television with the hope it would alleviate their fear. Soon it was time for bed, and everyone retired to their rooms. That night the oldest son, who slept downstairs, claimed he heard someone knocking at one in the morning on the door that led to the bathroom. Scared, he pulled the covers over his head. A minute or so later the boy felt someone sitting at the foot of the bed bouncing up and down on the mattress.

Then the covers were pulled off the boy, and the sheet "floated up into the air and onto the floor." The bed began to vibrate and bounce up and down with a "grinding noise."

He sat up in time to see a dark figure of a man wearing what looked like a top hat and long coat float from the bathroom door past his bed and up through the ceiling.

His parents had left three night lights on before they went to bed, but now they were all off. Terrified to leave the bedroom and walk in the dark house, he grabbed the sheet off the floor and pulled it over his head, shivering in fear. The episode for him was over, but upstairs his mother was about to have an experience she would remember for the rest of her life.

While sleeping with her husband by her side, the woman was awakened by the feeling of someone sitting on the bed. She tried to get up but could not move. She heard a voice say, "Get out of bed, get out of my room!" The voice then said, "Get out of my room, get out of bed, or you are going to have a heart attack!" The voice was that of a woman.

The wife tried in vain to wake her husband, but could only move her head and eyes slightly. To her shock she was paralyzed. The disembodied woman's voice continued to threaten her; it now said, "If you don't get out now, I will kill you and your family." Then the voice screamed in her ear, "*GET OUT!*" With this she was able to "snap" out of the paralysis and wake her husband. He seemed very tired and told her to go back to sleep, that it was just a dream.

She got up to check on the children. The boys in the next room seemed fast asleep, but she went downstairs and got very upset to find it dark with the night lights off. She ran into the bedroom of her eldest son, and he jumped up and yelled, "Help!" She turned on the light and saw that her son was pale. He told her about his experience and the "dark man with the hat" he had seen.

Being a very protective mother, she was deeply concerned that some evil force was trying to get them out of the house and the children were in danger. She sat with her son with the light on and was trying to decide if they should pack up and leave for a hotel.

During that time the father was still lying in bed awake, waiting for his wife to return to the room. Without warning the room became cold and the bed sheets were yanked off the bed. He told me in an interview: "I was really trying to play down the ghost thing, but that night convinced me that we were not alone in the house. After the sheets were pulled off I tried to pull them back, but my arms and legs would not move. It felt as if four people or creatures were holding my arms and legs and stretching them out. I yelled, '*Stop!*' When I yelled this word, my two sons in the next bedroom came running in, just in time to see their father pulled off the bed and onto the floor by some invisible force."

The family retreated to the living room, where they all sat around awake until dawn. That day they called the landlord, and he admitted that "strange things" did happen in the house. He told them his company used to have an office there, but the staff would not report to work because of a "number of unexplainable things that happened." He then had to move the office to the site of his construction business and began renting out the house.

The landlord explained to the couple that if they wanted to move, he would give them back their deposit. He always thought the strange stories of ghosts in the house were just tales from the overactive imaginations of the people who lived and worked there. The family found out later that neighbors who lived close by called the place "the old haunted house," since strange things had been seen and heard in the house and on the property for decades. However, the family had no place to go, and at least for now they would have to stay.

The next few days were rather quiet in comparison to what had taken place previously. There were still footsteps in the night; doors would be found open in the morning after they were closed; and there was still the feeling of an angry presence. The activity that seemed malicious in nature was confined to the upstairs, while the disturbances downstairs seemed benign and almost playful at times.

THE INVESTIGATION BEGINS

I was doing a radio show on a local station about UFOs when both witnesses called. They briefly explained about living in a "haunted house" and asked me if I could come over sometime to hear their story and take a look around. I explained that my primary interest was the investigation of encounters with Unidentified Flying Objects, but accepted their offer since it sounded too interesting to pass up. They both seemed sincere, so I gave them my phone number. They called me within twenty-four hours, and after a lengthy conversation I made an appointment to see them that weekend.

I arrived at the house late in the afternoon and was greeted by the couple and their dog. The children were sent to visit their grandmother, as the couple did not want them around while we toured the house and property and discussed ghosts and other types of paranormal phenomena.

As soon as I walked through the door I could sense something unsettling. The only thing that I can compare the feeling with is death. During my tour in the United States military, I spent time in Southeast Asia during the Vietnam War. After a firefight the tension remained in the air as the wounded were brought to our field hospital. It's hard to explain, but there was always a cold smell in the air that had a metallic-like odor to it, and this is what I smelled and sensed in this house—death.

As we walked into the dining room, two decorative metal plates that were hanging on the wall fell off and flew five feet across the room, almost hitting me. This was totally unexpected, and although I had witnessed poltergeist activity before, it never was personally directed at me. The couple picked up the plates, apologized, and told me that objects were thrown around quite frequently and they were getting used to it.

However, I was still not convinced that their experiences had a paranormal origin, since there were construction workers nearby who were blasting rock. It seemed more than a coincidence that the plates moved almost exactly the same time a blast was heard and felt. There are those paranormal investigators who believe the energy produced in a thunderstorm or even blasting is used by entities to manifest physical phenomena in our world. I am as skeptical today of this theory as I was back then.

The plates were secured to the wall using a hook. One would have to lift the plate up to get it off the wall. However, one thing could not be denied: both plates flew on their own power a considerable distance, and I appeared to be the target.

We then went upstairs; I felt a very noticeable drop in temperature as we entered the back bedroom. I looked around for the source of the cold air and found the closet with the "secret passage" in it. The cold air was definitely coming up from a tunnel that apparently went underground. It was impossible to explore this tunnel, because the floorboards that led to it were rotting and I would have fallen through the kitchen ceiling.

I wanted to look in the basement for evidence of animals, a bad furnace, faulty plumbing, or anything else that could possibly cause the noises the family heard at night. I knew that these things could not explain the voices or apparitions they all witnessed, but I wanted to see the foundation nevertheless. I also had to consider that perhaps the unexplainable manifestations could have been imagined and not real at all.

I went to the basement alone armed only with my flashlight. I opened the door and turned on the ceiling light. It was an unfinished basement and more like a root cellar with a dirt floor and stone walls. As I reached the center, the lights went out and the door closed with a bang. I was not expecting this and must admit it was very creepy standing in the dark. I switched on the flashlight, and after ten seconds the light dimmed as if the batteries were drained of energy. I found this very strange since they were fresh out of the package and installed that very day. Later, during future investigations, I would discover that DC power sources like batteries seem to drain quickly in locations where a strange phenomenon takes place.

Standing alone in the dark in a cold basement was not my idea of how an investigation should be conducted. I then carefully found my way to the door and was very surprised to find it locked. There was a slide bolt on the outside, and my first thought was that someone, perhaps the couple, had locked me in on purpose. This nonetheless did not explain the lights going out and the power drain in my flashlight.

I pounded on the door and yelled for someone to come and let me out. A minute or so later the couple came down to the cellar and unlatched the door. At the exact same time the door opened, the cellar lights came back on, but my flashlight was still dead. I tried slamming the door open and closed several times to see if it affected the lights; perhaps there was a loose bulb or faulty wiring, I thought. The lights stayed on and everything seemed normal. Also, the slamming of the door could not cause the bolt to slide in the locked position. The only way this could have happened is if someone or something pushed it.

The man of the house told me this happened quite frequently in the rear bedroom upstairs. They would walk into a room at night, turn on the light switch, and the door would slam shut and the lights would go off. I asked about the position of the light switch, and the couple said it would still be in the *on* position—and after about ten seconds the light would just come back on all by itself.

We went back upstairs and talked for a while over a cup of coffee. An arrangement was made for me to return the following weekend and continue my investigation. I wanted to do a background history of the house and find out who had lived there over the years since its construction. I also wanted to visit the local library and historical society to obtain information on the land before the house was built. I was also hoping the geology of the area would shed some light on this case.

NATIVE AMERICAN CONNECTION

After several hours of research, I found information indicating the property had a fascinating history. In the seventeenth century, on the exact physical location of the house, there was once a village of Native Americans.

Many American Indian tribes lived in what is now the state of Connecticut, including the Niantic, Pequot, Nipmuc, Mohegan, Mattabesic, and Paugusset. The Native American tribe that lived on the land in question before colonial settlers arrived was the Munsee.

The center of their village was once located about twenty meters from where the house was built. The Munsee way of life was spiritual and religious in nature. The Munsee shamans claimed direct contact with the spirits in the next world.

Although their language was similar to that of other Connecticut tribes and they shared many cultural similarities, the Munsee had their own leadership and territory. Many of their warlike neighbors seemed afraid to attack them for fear of reprisals from the spirits who guard their land.

European epidemics and conflicts with settlers eventually devastated the American Indians of the Northeast. The remaining tribes needed to merge with each other in order to survive. Today most Native Americans of Connecticut have heritage from more than one of these original tribes.

According to documents obtained at the Connecticut Historical Society in Hartford, the colonial settlers of the seventeenth century believed the land the Munsee lived on was cursed. This belief carried into the eighteenth century, and no one would build there. Evidently most of the former land of the Munsee became the town landfill.

My next task was to go to the town hall and scan through deeds and old newspaper clips. This was not an easy task, since many of the documents were faded or had pages missing. The investigation of the paranormal is not all exciting fieldwork; countless hours are spent doing research. Taking the time to find answers and obtain background information on a case separates the serious paranormal scientific investigator from the thrill seeker.

A TRAGIC HISTORY

I discovered that the house was built in 1789, and an additional bedroom was added downstairs in 1820. The property, which originally consisted of an area of land much larger than that immediately surrounding the house itself, was first owned by the Leeds family, who in 1826 sold it to a young couple in their early twenties by the name of George and Klara Louten. However, the Loutens only owned the house until 1830, when both of them were found dead there in November of that year. According to the report I found, the coroner assumed their deaths were due to suffocation caused by smoke from a faulty fireplace.

The police investigators were puzzled, however, as to why the couple was not in bed sleeping when they died. Klara was found upstairs in the bedroom in a nightgown, while George was found downstairs in his "day clothes." Normally with suffocation from a faulty fireplace, people died in their sleep. The report did not indicate whether or not the constable checked to see if the fireplaces had even been used that night.

The property was taken over by the state of Connecticut, which used part of the land as a garbage dump. In 1940 the state put the house and a small section of the original property up for sale, and it was purchased by the parents of the landlord who, many years later, rented the house to the modern-day couple.

However, as the landlord indicated, he and his family used the building as an office; they did not live there. A part of a beautiful rose garden on the east side of the house was also dug out and used as a parking area for trucks, since their family business was construction.

ALL THE RIGHT INGREDIENTS

It became apparent the house was built on land that had a history of paranormal activity dating back to the Native Americans. What was of great interest to me was the Munsee belief that part of their land was a gateway to another world. Today a garbage landfill can be found at the location of this gateway or portal to another reality. Also, the tragic deaths of the young couple in 1830 are what many ghost hunters call *a recipe for a haunting*.

The disembodied voices and the ghostly apparitions in the house were of a man and a woman. This was apparently more than a coincidence. Could it be that George and Klara never left after they died? The family who contacted me had no knowledge of the history of the property and neither did the landlord, so there is no way they could have imagined the spirits of a man and woman were causing the disturbances.

During my next meeting with the couple I told them of my findings. They were quite shocked. I withheld from them the names of the people who died in the house, since they were important in the next step of the investigation. I was going to conduct an experiment never tried in the house before—a séance!

From the analysis of the investigation and statements from the couple, it was apparent that if Klara and George were still in the house, she was restricted to the top floor and staircase while he seemed to favor the downstairs. For some reason Klara was angry and more malevolent toward the family, while George for the most part was playful and benign.

I asked the couple if it would be all right do a séance using a Ouija board with them present. I really didn't know how they would take this suggestion, since what most people know about the procedure has been restricted to over-dramatized and sometimes ridiculous presentations on television and in movies. They wanted to try anything that would help the situation, so they agreed. The séance was set for the next Saturday night, a time when the children would be staying with their grandparents. Those present would be the couple who owned the house, another married couple, and of course me.

THE SÉANCE

Let's face it: there is nothing scientific about a séance. If a human spirit was in the house, it might be aware that we would be trying to communicate with him or her. After the usual introductions and after going over what we expected to accomplish, we turned down the lights, lit a couple of candles, and took out my Ouija board, which I'd had for many years. I asked the couple to place their fingers on the planchette since they seemed to be the center of attention.

As soon as they touched the planchette, or pointer, it began moving around the board quickly. The couple said it felt like static electricity was running through their hair and arms. Then I asked that both of them take their hands off at the count of three: 1, 2, 3. To everyone's surprise the planchette kept on moving for at least two seconds after contact was released. I then asked them to place their fingers back on the planchette very lightly. Without hesitation it once again started to move quickly and erratically across the board. I then began to ask questions.

Phil: *Who are you?*

Response: *Spirit.*

Phil: *Are you Native American?*

Response: *No.*

Phil: *Then who are you?*

Response: *Ancient spirit god.*

Phil: *Do you live in the house?*

Response: *No house . . . my land . . . leave.*

Phil: *Are you responsible for the disturbances in the house?*

Response: *No. Others are . . . Goodbye.*

Phil: *We want to contact the spirits who are in the house.*

Response: *Hello.*

Phil: *Who are you? Give us your name.*

Response: *George.*

Phil: *Is your name George?*

Response: *Yes, you know that.*

Phil: *Were you married to Klara?*

Response: *Still, she killed me.*

Phil: *Why?*

Response: *Demon had control.*

Phil: *Is she still in the house?*

Response: *Yes, upstairs listening now.*

[Comment: This was quite incredible, since the couple did not know the names of the people who died in the house. Was the demon the Native American spirit-god who came through first? At that moment there was a noise upstairs like someone nervously walking back and forth. We all looked at each other, and the friends of the couple replied that they were getting freaked out because this was too strange. I then continued with the communication.]

Phil: *Klara, will you talk with us?*

At that point it sounded like someone came running down the stairs, stopped at the landing, and ran back up. I could not resist and had to investigate. I jumped out of my chair, ran to the base of the stairs, and looked up into the darkness. I got a very unsettled feeling, as if someone was at the top of the stairs in the dark looking back at me. There was a feeling of anger in the atmosphere that sent shivers up and down my spine. I felt as though I had been exposed to a field of static electricity. I decided to go back to the table and continue with the session.

Phil: *Klara, did you come down the stairs?*
Response: *She will not talk.*
Phil: *Why?*
Response: *Demon has control. Likes to hurt people.*
Phil: *Is this George?*
Response: *Yes. Not leave her here alone.*
Phil: *What can we do?*
Response: *Get demon to leave her before she hurts people.*
Phil: *How?*
Response: *Goodbye.*

At this point the communication stopped. We turned on the lights and discussed what had taken place. The friends of the couple advised them to leave the house for good before they themselves left quickly, saying, "This place is freaking us out!"

I stayed another two hours. Everything was quiet, and a peaceful feeling was felt in the house for the first time since the couple had moved in. I then left and asked the couple to contact me immediately any time of the day or night if the disturbances started up again.

A SHORT-LIVED PEACE

After my investigation and the evening of the séance all was quiet at the house, and the family seemed to go on with their normal lives. Then, two months later, I received a call from the husband, who was frantically saying that the children were waking up in the morning with scratches and bruises on their body. He also told me the oldest boy, who slept downstairs, woke up in the middle of the night on several occasions with a "serious bloody nose." It was so bad that once they had to take him to the emergency room.

The boy's father told me that they had called a priest at the local Catholic church to come and bless the house. After this the disturbances began again, and this time they seemed focused on the children. He told me they could not take any more and were moving out. They would be living with his parents in Stamford, Connecticut, until they found a new place.

I wasn't surprised to hear this and agreed with their decision, since children seem overly susceptible to the paranormal and it's not worth the risk to expose them to possible psychological and physical dangers.

Shortly after they moved out of the house, it was torn down by the owner and the land was sold to a business. Within months a three-story office building was constructed on the exact location where the house had stood.

Over the next five years the property would be sold twice, and today it remains vacant. Did the new owners also experience strange phenomena, and were they forced to move out? I don't know for sure, but a well-known organization was considering moving into the building yet declined to do so. Were they also scared away? I guess we will never know. Is the Native American spirit still on the land? More important, is it still holding the souls of George and Klara, and perhaps many others, captive?

CHAPTER 3

ANGRY AND FRIENDLY SPIRITS

A paranormal investigator must be very careful when talking with families who live in a house experiencing strange phenomena. This is true especially if children are present. I know of one case in which a self-proclaimed demonologist, after visiting a house, told the people living there a demon was in the house that had one goal in mind—to possess and kill their children. In this case the investigator continued to hound the family with telephone calls at all hours of the night. He would tell them in an excitable voice that the devil was going to kill them if they stayed another night in their home.

Finally, a lawsuit was filed against the investigator, since on more than one occasion he would wait for the family's children to leave school and attempt to "warn" them. He would run up to the two children before they got on their bus and terrify them with his paranoid and outlandish ideas.

The judge ruled in favor of the complainants but made it very clear that there is no law that regulates paranormal investigations. The judge did consider a charge of harassment and issued a restraining order against the investigator. He also ruled that if this person came before his court again on a similar charge, he would make sure there would be jail time.

A good number of people out there who are involved in the investigation of the paranormal are not stable. I know this for certain, because over the years quite a few of them have contacted me for one reason or another. It has always been my policy to work with people I know well or who have a solid reputation in the field.

In the field of paranormal study, those I do respect are few and far between. I judge researchers' ability by the contributions they've made in the field and not how many books they've written or the number of times they've appeared on television or the radio. Also, very rarely will I investigate a case with newcomers, since experience is lacking and they really don't know what they are getting into. I've worked on a case with a number of novice researchers who were traumatized with fear as a result of things that unfolded during an investigation. These experiences changed their lives, and I have always felt partially responsible.

In the past I have put a number of paranormal investigation teams together, and usually they don't last very long. In most cases, the individuals who join my team leave within a year because they realize much of the strange, bizarre stuff they read about in books or see on TV is very real and not something to be taken lightly. On the other hand, some investigations are interesting without the fear, and some are just downright funny.

FRIENDLY SPIRITS

In some circumstances that involve hauntings, the disturbances are benign and at times seem almost playful. Families and single people living in such a home often coexist with the "spirit" or entity that is manifesting the paranormal event. The experiencer will sometimes use the hauntings as the focus of a conversation or even throw a ghost party with their friends, with the hope that something will manifest and thrill their guests.

In many of these cases the individual or family living in the home may give the entity a pet name. If they hear a sound during the night, they might wake up and say, "Horatio, is that you?" If the person lives alone, they may talk to the entity as if it were an invisible roommate. They might say hello when entering the house and goodbye when leaving.

I have an example in my files in which the person would come home from a hard day at work and tell the entity how their day went and even ask for advice. Although they never received a direct answer, it did not discourage this person from continuing their conversation with the invisible being during the day and night.

From many alleged "hauntings" that I have investigated it is evident that a "ghost" can be an adult imaginary friend. It's interesting to note that the majority of these imaginary hauntings involve a woman who has a male specter or a man who has a female specter for a ghostly roommate.

It has been my experience that this type of individual really doesn't want the disturbances or entity to leave. They do, however, want validation from an investigator that there is something unusual going on in their home that cannot be explained in the conventional sense. They want to be able to tell their friends that "a real ghost hunter or paranormal investigator came to the house and said it was haunted."

However, in a case like this, if the entity is real and not imaginary, it often will attach itself to the person and will follow them wherever they relocate. In some cases the entity becomes jealous of lovers and other friends and wants the person all to themselves. If the person starts ignoring the entity, it may throw temper tantrums. For the most part these are harmless actions like throwing things around, pushing a glass off a table, or causing loud disturbances at night. In a case like this, the entity responsible behaves more like a spoiled child than a demonic monster.

I don't think anyone, no matter how experienced they are in investigating the paranormal, can say for sure who or what is responsible for activity in a house plagued by unseen forces. Most ghost hunters want to believe the cause of paranormal activity in a home is the result of a lost or angry human spirit—in other words, a ghost. However, over the years noted paranormal researchers, such as John Zaffis, have made it clear in their lectures and published papers that nonhuman entities may be responsible in a percentage of hauntings.

ANGRY SPIRITS

Human beings enjoy living a comfortable life. They like to be in control of their surroundings and feel secure. This is especially true in the home. However, what happens when your sacred place that you retreat to at the end of the day to relax is set in turmoil by unseen forces over which you have no control?

At first the individual or family will try to ignore what is taking place. If this doesn't work, then they will attempt to find a logical explanation for the events. When the paranormal disturbances get worse, they will often try to discuss them with a close friend or co-worker. Usually when they tell a confidant their house is haunted, they get a look of disbelief.

If the disturbances continue they will most likely seek the help of someone who will listen to them. At this point a scientist or paranormal investigator will be called with the hope of providing a rational answer or a sympathetic ear.

The majority of people who experience the paranormal in their home would just like it to go away. Sometimes the disturbances get so severe that they pack up their bags and leave the house, never to return.

In my files are eight instances in which a dream house was bought for an incredibly low price with a great deal of property in a beautiful part of the country away from the crowded city. The buyers then find out why there have been so many different owners and why the property was so cheap. Within a year of living in such a home, the owners are terrified by the events that take place and quickly put the house back on the market with a reduced price for a quick sale. The two case studies presented below are of an unseen malignant intelligence that seemed to have one purpose—to drive away all who lived there.

THE HAUNTED FARMHOUSE

Bethel, Connecticut, is one little haunted town. Many legends that date back to colonial times tell of vindictive witches who were put to death unjustly. There are also hundreds of old farmhouses in the area that were constructed before the Revolutionary War. Over the past several decades a number of owners of these old homes have contacted me regarding paranormal activity they have witnessed. The case selected for this book is a classic example of a haunting. The paranormal happenings were so severe that the owner had to move her children out of the house.

In the early winter of 1995 I received a call from my good friend Loretta Chaney. Loretta is a practicing psychic who resides with her husband, Scott, in Danbury, Connecticut.

Loretta told me of an old farmhouse in Bethel that was being plagued with some type of ghost. She mentioned that the owner would see apparitions during the night; physical objects would be thrown around; and the owner's two children, while asleep, had their bed sheets pulled off several times by some unseen force. Loretta asked me to visit the house with her and Scott to try and determine what was going on. She made it clear the owner wanted help, as she was ready to pack her bags and move out.

I listened carefully as Loretta related her psychic impressions of what was waiting for us. In the past I found that she had great insight into this other reality, and her counsel in these matters was always taken seriously by me and others who knew her.

Loretta said she felt that the spirit of someone who lived there a long time ago wanted to stay and be left alone. As a result, this force or entity was driving out everyone who moved in. This was true, since my initial research showed that the farmhouse had four previous owners in the past ten years.

We made arrangements to meet at the old house that Saturday. At the scene of the investigation would be Loretta, Scott, and my co-investigator at the time, Marianne Horrigan. Marianne had co-authored two books with me and in the past assisted on a number of investigations. I was confident that she would be an important part of this investigation.

We all arrived at the farmhouse in the early afternoon. The weather was not very cooperative: as soon as we pulled into the driveway it started snowing. Before we knocked on the door a quick examination of the property was done. Nothing really extraordinary was noticed. There was a partially built stone wall that Loretta felt was somehow tied to the activity in the house.

THE INVESTIGATION

After greeting the homeowner, a single mother with two children aged ten and fourteen, we walked into the house. She told us that her children would be staying with a friend during our visit so they would not be scared.

As soon as we stepped in, Loretta felt as if someone was watching and didn't want us there. The house was just on one level, and we made our initial survey in a matter of minutes. The owner, whom I'll call "Beth," said that on a number of occasions books on the shelf in the back room would go flying off the shelf. It usually happened when one person was alone in the room. Having heard this before, I asked the others to wait in the living room as I made my way to the back room, which was quite isolated from the rest of the house.

The room was dimly lit, and despite the heat blasting out of the radiator it seemed quite cold. The cold feeling increased, and it wasn't long until I could see my breath. Marianne yelled that she was going to join me when, all of a sudden, a book on the top shelf fell down and hit me on the head. This caught me by surprise, and my first thought was the ghost threw it at me. I regained my composure and looked for a logical explanation. Marianne then walked into the room, and I told her what had just taken place.

At the time I was standing close to the bookshelf. Perhaps this book was right on the edge, and Marianne walking into the room created vibrations that made it fall. Despite the stories of a book-throwing poltergeist in this room, I was not willing to accept that what had just taken place had a supernatural origin.

THE ATTIC

Beth mentioned that at night they could hear walking in the attic and what sounded like an elderly man choking or coughing. This usually took place at about two in the morning at least once a week. Scott suggested to Beth that the noises could be made by animals like squirrels and bats since many of the old houses in the area have to call pest control to get them out. Beth was sure it sounded like a human walking and making noises. She also said that several times a month she could hear the faint sound of a man up in the attic angrily using very "vile" curse words.

It was time to take a look in the attic. As I pulled down the attic stairs, Loretta and Scott refused to go up there with me. I slowly walked up with Marianne behind me when Loretta yelled out, "He knows you are coming up; he is waiting for you!"

After hearing this we froze in our tracks. I turned around and said to Marianne, "If something pushes me and I fall, will you catch me?" She didn't think I was serious, and her expression was one of amusement, not concern. We continued our trek up the steep flight of stairs and entered the darkness ahead.

The attic had no light. Luckily our flashlights were working properly, so we carefully began to investigate. As we got closer to a wall, it was apparent by the type of wood that this was not part of the original house. There was a small opening, and I shined my light through and was surprised to discover a small, hidden, room-like area.

The boards were loose, and with the permission of the owner we pulled them away. What we found surprised everyone. There was indeed a small room hidden behind the boards, complete with a mattress, a small table, a pitcher, and several glasses. Everything looked as though it hadn't been used in years. The room appeared to be some type of hiding place, but for whom?

We made our way back downstairs and told Beth about our discovery. She was both surprised and worried at what we'd found, since she was sure someone was up there. We assured Beth that the "room" had not been used in decades, and it appeared to have been sealed over with nails and wooden boards. I took one of the nails out of the boards and later found out it was similar to ones used around 1860. From this evidence we assumed that sometime in the mid-nineteenth century the small hiding place was sealed over. Loretta then suggested that we attempt to communicate with whatever was in the house.

CONTACT WITH AN ANGRY SPIRIT

We all sat on the floor in the living room and turned on one light. Loretta said that it might be possible for her to talk with the spirit that was causing the commotion in the house. She felt secure that her "guides" would protect her.

As Loretta prepared to make contact, the light went out. I then got up, flicked the switch a number of times, and the light came back on. A few seconds after I sat down, the light went out again. To this day it was never proven if there was a short in the circuit or if the entity was causing it. If some force was responsible, we were not going to play its game. I remained seated and told everyone to do the same. Loretta quickly made contact with the spirit and relayed what it was saying.

Loretta: *It's the spirit of an old man who died in the house and wants to be alone.*

Phil: *Did he die in the room in the attic?*

Loretta: *He said yes. It was a place that he used to hide out in. He said that all he wants is to be left alone and finish the wall outside.*

Phil: *Is that the wall we saw before we came in?*

Loretta: *He said yes. He wants us to leave.*

Phil: *There are people who live here.*

Loretta: *He is getting angry and says he wants them out, too. He will do whatever it takes to keep people out of his home.*

Phil: *Why don't you move on?*

Loretta: *He said, "To where? This is* **MY home!"**

Phil: *Go to the other side; loved ones must be waiting for you.*

Loretta: *He said he has no loved ones, and no one is waiting.*

Phil: *Can you live here and leave the people alone?*

Loretta: *No, he wants his privacy.*

Normally, in an investigation I do not act aggressively toward any entity causing the disturbance in a home, but in this case it was necessary, so I changed my tactics.

Phil: *I don't believe you are human. I think you are some entity that is just hiding out here.*

Loretta: *He said, "What do you think: I am a bug-eyed monster from outer space?"*

Phil: *If you can't live in peace with this family, then you will have to leave.*

Loretta: *He said, "Who is going to make me leave?" He called you an idiot and a wise-ass bastard.*

Phil: *I will write a story about this house and have it published in a major newspaper or magazine. Then you will get dozens of people coming around to look for you. There will be no peace and privacy.*
Loretta: *He said please don't do that.*
Phil: *I will if you are not respectful to those who live here.*

At that point the session ended. For whatever it's worth, I guess it worked, because from that night to the present day the old farmhouse has remained quiet, with no paranormal activity.

Was this a ghost or some other type of entity? I don't know for sure, but Loretta still feels today that it was the spirit of an old man who just won't leave his home and move on. Having a great deal of respect for her ability, I would have to say this is a strong possibility.

THE HOUSE OF DEATH

In the early spring of 2002 I was contacted by a middle-aged man who, after reading my book *Night Siege: The Hudson Valley UFO Sightings*, decided to track me down with the hope of finding a solution to a very unique problem he was facing.

The gentleman explained that he owned several old farmhouses in Putnam County, New York, which he rented out, but there was one property that he had trouble leasing.

For the first two minutes of the conversation he was very evasive concerning the nature of the problem. Finally, after considerable coaxing on my part, he just blurted out, "Everyone who moves into the house either dies or experiences some type of hardship, and I think it is haunted, cursed, or maybe possessed by some type of demonic force. Does this sound crazy?"

I told him it all sounded very interesting, and I didn't think he was crazy. I told him I had looked into many homes in that area that are thought to be haunted.

We made an appointment to meet the following weekend at a diner in Lake Carmel, which is located about five miles from the house in question. I asked the gentleman to bring documents on the house, along with its history if he had it. If not, I would have to go to the local town hall and retrieve the documents myself. This was a chore I would not have minded, since the clerk for Putnam County was a dear friend of mine. As it had been years since we had last talked, this would be a good excuse to visit him and combine business with pleasure.

We met at the diner at one p.m., and to my surprise he had two full folders packed with documents tracing the history of the house from its construction in 1810 to the present day. He told me that after all the strange things that went on in the house, he wanted to do some background research to find out what happened before he purchased the property.

What he discovered not only surprised him but was also, in his own words, "terrifying." We sat in the diner for the next two and half hours as the gentleman told me an amazing story using documentation to back up his incredible claims.

A DARK PAST

In the spring of 1810 the house was built by one Frederick Baddock over three acres of land. Baddock was thirty-seven at the time, married with two children. The documents state that he sold the property in 1816 to a John B. Denolda, who lived in the house with his wife and five children and started a small farm growing vegetables.

During the winter of 1817 his wife and three of his children died in the house; the cause was unknown. In January 1818 John, apparently depressed, sent his two living children away to spend the day with a relative. While they were gone he hanged himself in the attic.

The house remained vacant for almost ten years, apparently because of the deaths. In 1823 there were two newspaper accounts of the house being haunted. People who passed by heard screams coming from inside late at night. Ghostly apparitions "dressed in military uniforms" were also seen wandering around the property, walking or floating from the driveway to the basement door.

In 1827 the house was purchased by Stephen Sanunulet, who restored the old farmhouse and fixed the roof since there was considerable leaking.[4] Stephen lived in the house for nine months.

During the winter of 1827 his neighbors became concerned when no one had seen him in over a week. The town of Kent was small at the time, and people lived in a close-

---

4. The correct spelling of the last name was not clear, because the document suffered water damage. It appeared to be *Sanunulet*, or it could have been *Samunlat*.

knit community. Normally, if someone went away they would tell their neighbors or the local sheriff. His concerned neighbors went to his home and found the door unlatched. They found Stephen dead at the bottom of the stairs with a broken neck. The local coroner, a Dr. Marcus Heidenhall, ruled that he most likely tripped in the dark and ruled the death as an unfortunate accident.

Once again the house remained unoccupied, this time for twenty years. The locals considered the property haunted and bad luck since there had been so many deaths in a relatively short time. My research uncovered a newspaper clipping from the *Kent Journal*, dated 1839, which quoted a Kent Cliff resident who had seen unusual globes of light darting across the property. It was the opinion of the local minister that the lights were the spirits of the people who died in the house, and he told everyone to pray for them. Today we call this phenomenon "spook lights" or "ghost lights." However, back in the nineteenth century it was known as a *will o' the wisp*.

At the time, *will o' the wisp* was the most common name given to mysterious lights that were said to appear around places that were haunted. The phenomenon seems most common during the spring, especially around marshes. There are a great number of nonscientific explanations for will o' the wisps: the most common is that they are malevolent spirits of the dead or are demonic in nature. In modern times, the strange lights are often thought to be associated with UFOs.

During the colonial period in America, the will o' the wisp was associated with spirits of the dead who could not enter either Heaven or Hell and were doomed to malignantly wander the reality of the living. The lights were also thought to be omens of death, and when they were seen in graveyards they were often called "corpse lights." Corpse lights were believed to light the path of a coming funeral from the deceased person's home to the graveyard in the form of small flickering flames. In other tales, the appearance of the lights were thought to be bad luck and often said to manifest in places where a tragedy was about to occur.

The phenomenon is very real and has been documented at many different locations in southern New York for over two hundred years. Science explains the will o' the wisp or ghost light phenomenon as being caused by marsh gas—formed from rotting vegetation. As the gas rises into the air, the oxygen ignites it, creating a ball of glowing light or sometimes a flame. The colors vary considerably, but the most common one is yellow.

It was clear from what I was told and read in the documents that a will o' the wisp or ghost lights were seen on the property since the construction of the house. I had to consider the simple fact that a misinterpreted natural phenomenon may have triggered the many ghost stories.

From the mid-1800s until about 1910 the records are not clear, and it is uncertain who owned the property during this time period. The land was farmed, but the house remained vacant. Shortly after World War II the parents of the present owner purchased the house with the hope of renting it, since there was a considerable call for "country" homes by well-to-do families living in New York City. The house was repaired and electricity was added, as well as plumbing.

The current owner told me during our lunch at the diner, "I heard stories from my grandfather and parents that when they went into the house they would hear sounds like children crying upstairs and noises as if someone was walking around on the top floor and attic. My grandfather said that on one evening in 1946, while he was locking up after the electrician was leaving, he heard a noise outside like a man yelling in pain. Thinking that someone was injured on the property, he went around the back of the house and saw two men who looked 'battle wounded' with bandages around their heads and arms, slowly walking into the root cellar. He asked them if they needed help, but the men continued walking, as if they were deaf. My grandfather watched them walk into the root cellar, and when he turned the corner to catch up to the men, they were gone. He said they didn't look like ghosts; they were solid like real people."

After I asked him a number of questions for my clarification, the current owner continued with his story: "My grandfather said it was very strange, since they were dressed in what he called 'uniforms of the Continental Army.' To the day he died he believed he saw the ghosts of injured American soldiers from the Revolutionary War."

THE HAUNTED "ROOT CELLAR"

I asked the owner about the so-called root cellar, since what was described to me sounded more like one of the ancient

"Druid" stone chambers found in that section of New York. The stone chambers are now thought to be ancient structures built centuries before the northeastern United States was settled by Europeans.

He then showed me a picture, and there was no doubt what I was seeing. The "root cellar" was a cylindrically shaped stone chamber. What was even more surprising is it was used as part of the building foundation. This was the third time I have seen this in the Putnam County area. In my opinion, there is no coincidence: all three houses that were built on top of a stone chamber have a history of strange phenomena and bad luck to all who live in them.

This really sparked my interest, as I have been studying these structures since the early 1980s. My research has appeared in a number of publications, including the New York *Daily News Sunday Magazine* and the *New York Times*.

According to local folklore, during the Revolutionary War wounded or ill soldiers were kept in the stone chambers until they got well or died. During the 1860s some of the chambers were used by the local undertaker in the winter to store bodies before burial. Whether or not this particular chamber was used for any similar purpose is unknown. With a history like this, you can understand why the local old-timers considered the stone chambers haunted or bad luck.

After seeing the picture of the so-called root cellar, I had wanted to plan an onsite investigation very soon. However, before a date could be set up, the gentleman continued with the history of the house.

During the 1960s, '70s, and '80s, a total of eight families rented the house. They all left within one year. One family claimed they heard noises at night like someone running up and down the stairs with heavy boots on. This would wake them up at night and create considerable fear in the family. This paranormal occurrence was so frequent that it terrified their children, so the family moved out.

He then told me that "all the people who rent the house reported the same thing: noises and crying in the house in the middle of the night that scared them out. Also, couples who move in end up fighting with each other and in two cases got divorced. The house must have some type of evil presence, since if you stay a long time it brings out the anger in people. I know this sounds crazy, but I believe that something in the house triggers off the negative emotions in people and feeds off of them."

I told him that I'd heard of this before. There are paranormal investigators, including myself, who believe there are entities that feed on negative emotions and get stronger. As he listened, his eyes began to tear up as if he was reliving some tragic event. The gentleman then began to tell me about his night in the house. As he slowly got into the story, his voice started to shake, apparently out of fear. He gave me permission to use the story, provided his last name and the address of the property are not used. His amazing story appears below as it was told to me.

THE HANGING MAN

"For years I heard about the strange occurrences that took place in the house. I knew there was something going on because, let's face it, too many people said they saw ghosts, including my relatives. The house has been vacant over the past several years so I decided to find out if any of the stories were true. Armed with a thermos of hot coffee and a sleeping bag, I planned to spend the night. I got there at just about sunset; it was July 12, last year.[5] I also brought a radio to listen to some music and planned to stay most of the night. My plans were to leave at about two a.m. if nothing strange happened.

"At eleven p.m. I was taking a walk outside near the front entrance when I heard crying coming from the upstairs. The window was open, and it sounded like one or two small children crying because they were unhappy. I then put my flashlight on and ran upstairs into the bedroom, but nothing. I said to myself, 'What the hell?' and went downstairs. As soon as I reached the lower level there was a sound like the whooshing of wind near the stairs. Then, while I stood in the dark, a horrible sound came from the stairs, as if someone had fallen. It sounded like a real heavy man. I ran to the stairs and put on the lights and saw nothing. Then a sound came from what I thought was upstairs. I ran upstairs and saw nothing. I then heard another sound that was like a thumping; it was coming from the attic. I went up the small steps that led to the attic door and opened it. I was shocked to see a man hanging from the beams. It looked like he had

_____
5. The year was 2001.

hanged himself. Now the vision, ghost, or whatever it was only lasted for a second, but I know it was real.

"After the hanging man vanished I ran downstairs, out the door and into my car, and I took off for home. When I arrived home my wife saw that something was wrong and asked me what was going on. I told her about the things that happened in the old house, and she said something like 'See, I told you the place was haunted.' Anyway, since that time I haven't had the courage to go back. The place is now for sale real cheap. I have a realtor handling the property. So far there have been quite a few people looking at it, but no buyers."

I asked him a number of questions to clarify a few of the things he told me. It was my opinion that this individual was telling the truth and recounting a past experience that visibly upset him. I then asked to visit the place and got permission to spend the night. He gave me directions and a key and said I would have to go alone.

MY VISIT

I arrived at the house late on a cloudy Sunday afternoon in mid-spring. The property was quite isolated, and the nearest house was about three hundred yards away. As I got out of my car, I looked at the windows and thought I saw the image of a man looking out from the top floor. It only lasted a second, and I chalked it up to the reflection of nearby trees whose branches were swaying in the wind.

The windows looked very dark, and I must admit that the place appeared very spooky. I walked around the property and noticed clumps of decayed vegetation on the north side in what apparently was a marsh. This was located about twenty-five yards from the house, and there was a distinct smell of decaying vegetation. As it rises from the ground, it could ignite when it hits oxygen in the air. When this takes place, a popping sound can be heard and the gas will burn with a green or yellow glow. I thought that perhaps this could account for the stories of ghost lights that are seen around the property by owners, neighbors, and people who pass by.

Next, I walked to the back of the house, because I wanted to see the stone chamber that was used as a foundation for the structure. I was not disappointed; it was a real stone chamber. The owner put a door on the entrance, which was locked; however, he had given me the key. I opened the padlock. The chamber was quite large inside and cylindrical in shape.

In 1983, when my research began on the stone chambers of New York, I discovered there are two basic shapes: cylindrical and oval. To the builders of the chambers the two shapes may have represented male and female energy.

I walked in and noticed a layer of mortar on the walls, filling in the spaces between the rocks that were slowly crumbling, composed of limestone and sand. This mixture was common in the eighteenth to mid-nineteenth centuries. The chamber was about thirty feet in length and the height was more than six feet. I knew this because I could walk the entire length without having to bend down.

The chamber was dark and cold, and I felt as if something was with me in there. It was amazing how the builders positioned the house so that most of the weight rested on the roof of the chamber, which was made up of slabs of cut granite. The stone chambers seem to draw the paranormal like a magnet, and it was evident to me why this house had so many deaths and strange happenings.

STAKEOUT

The sun was now low in the sky. I left the chamber and entered the house through the front door. My plan was to spend the night to see if the hauntings were real or just the product of overactive imaginations.

There was no furniture in the house, but the electricity was still on. As it got dark I settled in. My first task was to set up my camera loaded with blue-sensitive film on a tripod. My previous research indicated that most paranormal phenomena emit in the blue, rather than the red, end of the spectrum. I positioned the tripod near the stairs and set the shutter speed to time exposure. I was hoping to catch an image of the phantom that had been seen and heard falling down the stairs.

Next on the agenda was to take a look around. The downstairs seemed quite ordinary: a kitchen, a living room, and a dining room. The upstairs had two bedrooms and a hallway that led to a full bathroom.

Continuing my exploration, I found the stairs leading to the attic. It was here the hanging man was reported, so I was eager to take a look around. I reached the attic and was quite startled—it was the home for an undetermined number of bats. I now thought perhaps the sounds people often reported coming from the attic were caused by bats and not ghosts. Since the flying creatures seemed upset by my presence, I left for the downstairs to begin my all-night vigil.

The house was quiet as it got darker. The only sound came from the top floor, which I thought was the attic. It sounded like the bats were ready to leave and fly out of the vent to hunt for their evening meal of insects. They did make a racket, and I could understand why it alarmed past residents. With a little imagination, their screeching could have been mistaken for little children crying. As the sun slowly set there were no ghosts or dimensional beings making themselves known in the house, just bats in the belfry.

As the hours passed, it became apparent to me this just might be a waste of time. However, if there were some type of interdimensional entity on this property, it must have known why I was there. It surely would not put on a show for me. It most likely would remain quiet, not wanting to draw attention to itself.

With my sleeping blanket around me, I slowly drifted off into a light sleep.

All was quiet. Then without warning I awoke, startled to hear a loud sound like a heavy body falling down the stairs. I jumped up and went for the light switch, but the lights would not turn on. I switched on my flashlight and pointed it at the stairs, but saw nothing. My camera and tripod was still at the base of the stairs, undisturbed. If something physical did indeed fall down the stairs, it would have surely knocked over the camera.

I then ran upstairs, checked all the rooms and finally the attic, but found nothing. There was no doubt in my mind that something big and heavy rolled down those stairs. With my excitement now controlled, the concern and fear that was slowly growing within me faded. Yes, I admit my first thought was to get the hell out of there, especially after the power failure.

If this was a real paranormal event, then how could I just leave the house? It would be quite embarrassing when the case was presented to say, "I don't know what happened after that, because I ran out the door." I began to take pictures of the stairs and the surrounding rooms. After the initial excitement wore off, I settled down once again on the floor.

The time was now three a.m., only three hours until sunrise. Needless to say, sleep did not come to me, but the rest of the night was quiet. At the break of dawn I packed up my equipment in the car and went home.

FOLLOW-UP

I arrived home, went over my notes, and pulled out some of the news clippings about the so-called ghost lights on the property. I was pretty sure that what people reported as "spirits" on the land could have been explained by gases from decaying plants in the marsh igniting with oxygen. I had seen this phenomenon several times before during earlier investigations, and from a distance it does look very ghostly.

What convinced me most was that the dates of the reports of the ghost lights were all in late March and April. In southern New York, the ground will usually stay frozen until early

March. During this time dead vegetation is trapped under the ground or frozen just above the surface. As the ground thaws, the plants begin to decay at a quick rate and a gas is released. The gas then ignites in the air just above the ground. If there is a slight wind the glowing gas may move and then dissipate. At times the burning gas can take an elongated shape. If you let your imagination run wild, when viewed at a distance in the dark it may seem like a human form.

There were several things from the reports that didn't make sense. A few of the witnesses who saw the spook light on the property said it was in the shape of a sphere and that it moved away from the marsh area down across the lawn and near the bottom of the driveway, where it vanished. I have never heard of glowing marsh gas traveling this distance from the source of origin. If we take into account that the witnesses were relating the facts as they actually took place, then some of the ghost-light sightings remained a mystery.

During my stay at the house the power went out. There were no other homes within my view and no street light outside. I wondered if the power outage could have been the result of a paranormal event. In the past, researchers, including me, have experienced a loss of electrical power in a home that was experiencing paranormal activity. I then called Con Edison, the local power company, and I was told that there was indeed a power outage at that location from one to four a.m. caused by a blown transformer.

It was very coincidental the transformer should blow the night I chose to stay in the house. I doubt if some other-worldly force went out of its way and knocked out everyone's lights in the neighborhood just to spook me. However, as a great and wise Buddhist priest once told me, "There is no such thing as a coincidence."

The loud noise I heard by the stairs troubled me, and although the sound was captured on my recorder it was inconclusive evidence. Having access to a darkroom, I developed the film right away. To my disappointment, most of the frames were blank, except for one. The frame showed a dark large spherical blob on the negative. Since this was black-and-white film, the print should show a white lighted source with a dark background.

My readers must remember I was using blue-sensitive film, no flash, with time exposures of one minute for each of the ten frames. The blob of light was at least the size of a soccer ball, and its position would have been in the middle of the stairs. I saw nothing visually, but the noise was so loud that it did startle me. The noise on the stairs could have been connected to the image captured on film, but I can't say for sure. The blob of light was just outside the range of human eyesight, but very prominent in the blue and ultraviolet end of the electromagnetic spectrum.

I had investigated eight cases before this one in which spook or ghost lights entered a home and caused physical phenomena such as knocking over lamps on tables, exploding light bulbs, breaking glass, and making a loud crashing noise as they hit a wall or ceiling. Was it possible this caused the crashing noise on the stairs?

My research has shown that not all ghost lights are visible to the naked eye, yet at times they are able to exert a significant force on physical objects. There are five reports in my file in which people and animals have been burned by being in close proximity to ghost lights.

Some researchers believe that so-called ghost or spook lights are electrostatic discharges that originate in the lower atmosphere, comparing the phenomenon with ball lightning.

Ball lightning is an atmospheric phenomenon about which science knows very little. The term refers to reports of glowing, usually spherical objects that vary from pea-sized to several meters in diameter. Many of the early reports say ball lightning sometimes explodes, leaving behind the odor of sulfur. This could be the reason why it was often associated with manifestations of the devil or an evil spirit.

There are records of ball lightning forming in the absence of thunderstorm activity. One recent theory suggests it is produced by the ionization of air and by alpha particles during radon decay in the dusty atmosphere.[6]

In the 1980s the Environmental Protection Agency discovered that many homes in Putnam County, New York, had high levels of radon gas in their basements. The problem is so widespread that a homeowner must have an up-to-date radon gas test before they can sell a property in the county.

---

6. An alpha particle is composed of two neutrons and two protons. It has a total charge of +2. It is a nucleus of helium and often detected in the natural radioactive decay of many isotopes.

Laboratory experiments with high voltage have produced effects that are visually similar to reports of ball lightning, but it is presently unknown whether these are actually related to any naturally occurring phenomenon. Scientific data on natural ball lightning are scarce, owing to its infrequency and unpredictability.

After my experience at the house, it was clear that if some poltergeists are caused by a natural electrostatic discharge we cannot see, then many paranormal investigators, including the many so-called ghost hunters, might consider revaluating their cases.

Although I could not explain the many reports of ghostly apparitions that people have seen in and outside the house, some of the so-called paranormal events reported over the decades could have natural explanations.

Finally, there was the stone chamber on the property. These structures have always have been associated with all aspects of the paranormal. Native Americans in the area believed they were built by an ancient people to mark a doorway that connected our world with another reality.

All the strange occurrences at the old home in Putnam County cannot be explained by our current command of scientific knowledge. I really have no explanation for what I heard at the stairs during my stakeout that night.

Paranormal events continue to take place at the house, and to my knowledge the owners have had no luck selling or even renting the property. Their next step is to level the home and sell the land to a prospective builder. However, from my experience this is no guarantee that the "hauntings" will stop. In a number of similar cases, when the original structure was torn down and a new one constructed, the paranormal events continued. In some instances they even escalated.

If the house is torn down, it would also mean the stone chamber will be destroyed. They are structures that are lost in time. They are a legacy of an unknown people and a very important part of the history of New York and most of New England.

Were there a number of ghosts in the house, or was it just all some strange type of natural phenomena? My investigation on this matter is inconclusive, but one thing is for sure: I could not explain everything that I and others witnessed in the House of Death.

CHAPTER 4

GHOSTS OF SLEEPY HOLLOW

Electronic voice phenomena (EVP) are electronically gener-ated noises that sound like human speech. EVP have been picked up using radios, computers, and of course audio re-corders. It seems when the changeover to digital took place, recordings of EVP increased considerably.

In the past I had always been quite skeptical of EVP, but when I began receiving them on electronic equipment during a recent investigation, my opinion of their validity changed. Also, I began experimenting with rapid-scan radio EVP,[7] and the amount of information I have been able to receive during my research is quite convincing.

Paranormal investigators believe that EVP originate from a spirit or ghost of a human being who has not fully passed over to the other side. My research has shown that EVP are most likely produced by a number of different

---

7. Also called a "franks box," "ghost box," or "MiniBox."

communicators—some human, some not. The bottom line is that no one really knows who is talking at the other end or how it's done.

To actually obtain EVP on a tape recorder using magnetic heads is exciting, since it means that the "signal" generated by the "communicator" was electromagnetic in nature. In the early 1980s I was able to obtain EVP while visiting one of the most haunted towns in New York State—Sleepy Hollow!

This haunted hamlet is located on the east side of the Hudson River, about twenty-five miles from the heart of New York City. The village was settled originally by the Dutch in the mid-1600s, who elected to call their new home *Slapershaven*, or *Sleeper's Haven* in English. There are still many residents of the village who are descendants of the original Dutch settlers.

Washington Irving, who lived from 1783 until 1859, called the then-secluded village *Sleepy Hollow* in his classic story "The Legend of Sleepy Hollow." This was probably done to help protect the true identity of the characters in his story, but no one knows for sure.

In 1996, the town's name, at that point North Tarrytown, was officially changed to Sleepy Hollow, because the local chamber of commerce thought it would be good for tourism. They were right. A short time after the official name change, Sleepy Hollow became a very exclusive place to live and a popular place to visit, with a blending of the old world and modern design.

Walking down the town's main street, you can have lunch or dinner at establishments named for characters in Washington Irving's tales. If you are brave enough, you can also take a daytime or nighttime stroll across the Headless Horseman Bridge. This is the famous bridge across which the ghost could not cross. The bridge was named sometime after the publication of Irving's story, but no living historian in the town seems to know exactly when. Today approximately ten thousand people live in Sleepy Hollow, as well as a great number of friendly and nasty disembodied spirits.

What most people don't know is that Washington Irving based his stories on old legends and actual people. When he wrote his short story "Rip Van Winkle," Irving was fascinated by the many folklore stories of gnomes in the Catskill Mountains who came into our world every twenty years to party and play nine-pins on the mountaintops. After Irving heard about the legend of the great explorer Henry Hudson's encounter with the gnomes in 1609, he was inspired to write the tale of Rip Van Winkle. Today there are people who live in the Catskills who claim they are the descendants of Rip Van Winkle and that the story was actually based on a real person.

Since I live within a one-hour drive of Sleepy Hollow, my adventures into investigating paranormal events, especially UFOs, have taken me there on many occasions. Sleepy Hollow is considered by paranormal investigators worldwide to be one of the most haunted locations in North America. After all, it is the birthplace of Irving's tale "The Legend of

Sleepy Hollow," which features the greatest phantom of all time—the infamous *Headless Horseman*.

Here is how Washington Irving describes the Headless Horseman: "The dominant spirit . . . that haunts this enchanted region, and seems to be commander-in-chief of all the powers of the air, is the apparition of a figure on horseback, without a head. It is said by some to be the ghost of a Hessian trooper, whose head had been carried away by a cannonball . . . and who is ever and anon seen by the country-folk hurrying along in the gloom of night, as if on the wings of the wind. His haunts are not confined to the valley, but extend at times to the adjacent roads, and especially to the vicinity of a church at no great distance . . . The ghost rides forth to the scene of battle in nightly quest of his head, and the rushing speed with which he sometimes passes along the Hollow, like a midnight blast, is owing to his being belated, and in a hurry to get back to the churchyard before daybreak."[8]

"The Legend of Sleepy Hollow" is believed to be based on real facts, legends, and actual people who lived in the town who encountered the ghostly apparition. It is a documented fact that Irving did indeed name the main character of the story after an Army officer whom he met in 1814, by the name of Ichabod Crane.

It seems that Irving was amused at Captain Crane's extraordinary fear of ghosts. For some reason he used the officer's real name instead of changing it. Some historians think he just liked the name. Other historians believe the

---

8. Washington Irving, "The Legend of Sleepy Hollow." First published in 1820.

character in the legend was based on Jesse Merwin, who taught at a local schoolhouse in Kinderhook, New York, where Irving spent six months.[9] It is possible that the personality of Ichabod Crane was based on both men—only Washington Irving knows for sure, and he is not talking.

The character of Katrina Van Tassel is thought to have been based on a real woman, Catriena Ecker Van Tessel. The Van Tessel family descendants still live in Tarrytown, and the headstones of family members can be found in the Sleepy Hollow Cemetery.

Since I introduced this chapter with the infamous Headless Horseman, that's a good place to start. There have been periodic sightings of the ghost and his horse for the better part of two hundred years, a few of them in the twentieth century. To the old-timers in Sleepy Hollow, he is much more than just a legend.

ON THE TRAIL OF THE HEADLESS HORSEMAN

I arrived at Sleepy Hollow on a sunny, brisk fall day just before Halloween in 1986. Although I had driven through the area of Tarrytown on many occasions before, this would be my first visit to Sleepy Hollow to conduct an investigation. My plan was to spend at least two days in the town, so I checked into a hotel in Tarrytown to set up my base of operations. After settling in my room, my first stop would be

---

9. *Life and Letters of Washington Irving* (New York: G. P. Putnam, 1869), vol. 3, 185–86.

Tarrytown's local historical society and then the library in an attempt to separate fact from fantasy.

My first day was spent doing research, and I found out a number of amazing facts. The first bit of information that really surprised me was that the Headless Horseman was not something invented from the imagination of Washington Irving. The story was based on a tale that originated just after the Revolutionary War. What follows is a summary of that tale:

"The headless horseman was a Prussian-Hessian soldier who fought against the Americans. During the war, the Horseman was one of 580 Hessians killed in the battle at Chatterton Hill near Tarrytown.[10] During the fighting his head was blown off from cannon fire. He was buried in a graveyard near the Old Dutch Church alongside a very old oak tree. His ghost was seen during the fall every year after that carrying the cannonball. Unlike most specters, the Horseman was feared, since he was often seen carrying a sword and would attack the living who had the unfortunate luck of running into him. The Horseman returns from the land of the dead on All Hallows' Eve to search for his head. Only after he finds it can he rest.

"In 1780 a man encountered the horseman returning from a trip to his home in the Hollow. The horseman made him climb on his horse, and together they rode through bushes and walls. When they reached the bridge, the horse-

---

10. Also called the Battle of White Plains, this was a battle in the American Revolutionary War fought on October 28, 1776, at White Plains and Tarrytown, on Chatterton Hill. The invading British army had a large number of Hessian soldiers.

man turned into a skeleton. The man then fell off the horse, and the horseman disappeared in a clap of thunder."[11]

My first task was to find the Old Dutch cemetery. This is allegedly the place where the Horseman was buried. There wasn't much to go on except that the body was placed in an unmarked grave near a large old oak tree. Also, I wondered what they did with the other five-hundred-plus Hessians who died in the battle. Further research indicated most of them were buried in the area or burned; however, some of them, including my old friend the Horseman, were buried in Sleepy Hollow.

I left the library and drove to the Sleepy Hollow Cemetery. Locating the final resting place of the infamous phantom would be like finding a needle in a haystack, since no one knew the name of the Horseman. The Sleepy Hollow Cemetery is not the Old Dutch cemetery. Many people who visit this area on Halloween make this mistake. The Old Dutch graveyard is attached to the Sleepy Hollow Cemetery but is located deeper in the woods.

I parked my car and began to walk through the cemetery. Many of the stones were modern, but some did date back to the eighteenth and nineteenth centuries. I stopped at the grave of Washington Irving and thought about what the area looked like in his day.

I noticed a woman just ahead of me with her young daughter, who was perhaps six years old. I approached the woman, and we talked for a while. I introduced myself as

---

11. This story was recorded by Johann Karl August Musäus in late 1781, but the original author is unknown.

a scientist and paranormal investigator who was doing research on the ghostly legends of Sleepy Hollow. The woman was a resident of nearby White Plains, but she had never been to Sleepy Hollow before. As a child she read Washington Irving's story and wanted to finally see the town for herself.

She told me a friend was driving down Route 9 (North Broadway) past the cemetery at night and saw five human phantoms running through the woods in single file. Her friend described them as being transparent, and the "ghosts" were able to run right through the gravestones and the bushes. The apparitions then disappeared into a wooded area. She also told me that, according to her friend, the "ghosts" were all men and dressed in uniforms. She thought they were the spirits of British soldiers killed in the Revolutionary War because they had "red coats."

The young woman then mentioned that when she and her daughter, Melissa, entered the graveyard that day, Melissa repeatedly heard the voice of a young girl saying hello. Melissa then ran to the grave of a girl who had died in 1898, at the age of only ten. Melissa told her mother, "This is the little girl who keeps calling me." I asked Melissa if she still heard the voice. While hiding behind her mother, she shyly said no. We then went our separate ways; my next stop was the Old Dutch cemetery to search for the graves of the Hessians killed in battle and the Headless Horseman.

A VERY SPOOKY PLACE

Even in the daytime, the Sleepy Hollow Cemetery is a spooky place. As I walked farther from the road, the gravestones got older. Continuing my walk I came to a small stone wall and climbed over it. I realized that I was now in the Old Dutch cemetery, since some of the stones dated back to the seventeenth century. I looked around for familiar names that came up in my research, but the headstones were so weathered that most of them were impossible to read.

I came upon ground that looked like it was slowly caving in. If a large hole or pit is dug, there is always air between the dirt as it is filled in. If bodies are thrown in the pit, there are even more spaces where pockets of air can be trapped. It was apparent to me I was looking at a gravesite where a number of bodies were quickly buried in a large, hastily dug pit.

About ten yards to the right was a large, dead oak tree that had been hollowed out by insects and animals. Could this be the oak tree mentioned in the legend? Was this the location of the burial place of the Horseman? If this was true, then it seems the famous phantom was not buried alone but rather with an unknown number of other soldiers who were also killed during the Battle of White Plains.

I continued my exploration of the rest of the graveyard and the woods nearby, but found nothing else. There was an eerie, unpleasant feeling in the atmosphere, cold like death. Although there was no fear, I couldn't wait to get out of there and back to my car and return to the comfort of my hotel room.

THE NEXT STEP

It was late afternoon, and I decided to walk around town and perhaps get a bite to eat. I also wanted to ask local residents about sightings of the Horseman or any other paranormal events people witnessed. I stopped at a diner for an early dinner and asked the waitress if she knew anybody in town who'd had a paranormal experience. I told her that I was a scientific researcher and was gathering information. She told me she knew for sure that a great number of people saw a giant UFO pass over the town back in 1983 and 1984. The waitress was referring to the sightings of the Hudson Valley UFO, which I wrote about in *Night Siege*.

Despite my many questions, she was patient. I then asked her if anyone had seen the Horseman. She laughed and said, "That's just a story, or people think it is. It was so long ago, and nobody actually knows if the thing is real or not."

The waitress told me some years ago there was a story going around that a number of people saw the Headless Horseman riding through the old cemetery. She insisted these people were serious about it, and the story was carried in one of the local papers.[12] Then she mentioned the police said it was just someone playing a Halloween joke by riding a horse in a costume, but no one was ever caught.

After lunch I visited the local police, who said they get calls every Halloween night about some joker on a black horse riding through the Old Dutch graveyard. The officer then laughed and said, "You don't really believe in

---

12. I could not find the story despite a detailed search at the local library looking through papers published during the previous years.

that nonsense, do you?" After a short explanation of my research the police took my number and said half-jokingly, "If we get any more Horseman sightings, we'll call you." As of the writing of this book, not one call has been made to me from the Tarrytown Police.

THE NIGHT STALKER

The town of Sleepy Hollow is very beautiful in the fall and rich in early American colonial history. Also, as one would expect, Halloween is considered to be a major holiday, and during my visit the town was very nicely decorated. It seems that Halloween draws a considerable number of tourists, and the town does very well during this ultimate spooky time of the year.

I visited all of the historical sites and obtained a considerable amount of information on many haunted local locations and legends. Next on my agenda was to go back to the Old Dutch cemetery after dark. This was not a pleasant thought, since the place was spooky enough during the day.

After dinner the sky started to darken, and I once again made my way to the Old Dutch Church, the Headless Horseman Bridge, and finally the Old Dutch graveyard. The night was clear with a crescent moon in the sky and, despite it being the end of October, the temperature was a mild fifty-two degrees.

The only equipment in my possession was a flashlight, tape recorder, and my trusty camera. The wind started to pick up, and I heard a strange creaking noise in the dark close by the woods. The creaking sound was eerie and caught me by surprise, but I realized it was nothing more than tree branches rubbing together in the wind.

It was somewhat strange the wind should pick up at that moment. I started recording my data and moved around the suspicious-looking pit that was discovered earlier. With the wind starting to actually howl, there were a number of times when I had to stop and listen because it sounded like a human voice. After one hour of exploring, the temperature dropped quickly. This seemed quite unnatural. There was a strange feeling in the air; it felt as if someone was in the dark watching me.

The feelings of being watched were justified because, when I turned around, about thirty yards away was the figure of a man standing in the Sleepy Hollow Cemetery. He appeared to be looking in my direction, which was a little unsettling. Turning my glance away from this man, I began to walk away.

As I turned around, once again there were now two figures standing in the same place. They were just standing there motionless in the dark; I could not make out any features. They looked to be about six feet tall. The strangest thing was they appeared to be wearing the same clothes. This made them look like identical shadow twins.

They then started walking in my direction very fast. This was a little unnerving, so I circled around them through the dark woods and finally made it back to my car, got in, and turned on the headlights. I waited for several minutes expecting the shadow men to emerge from the woods, but nothing was seen.

It was time to end my nighttime adventure and head back to the hotel. While driving I wondered who the strange shadow men might have been and why they showed an interest in me. During my encounter with the shadow men, my feeling was that I was violating their space and they wanted me to leave.

THE VOICE

After arriving back at the hotel, my mind began to race with thoughts of what had taken place at the Old Dutch cemetery. Who were the two strange men? Were they ghosts, spirits, or just two ordinary people taking a late stroll in the graveyard? One thing was for certain: my inner voice that had saved me many a time during my military service was clearly saying, *"Get out of here now!"*

I had taken a considerable number of pictures and was anxious to find out if anything paranormal was caught on film. This was in the era before digital photography, and with my darkroom not in operation at the time I would have to wait a week before the photos returned from the processing lab. Using a small cassette recorder I was able to keep track of my activities and made notes during the investigation. I played back the tape and, to my surprise, while near the pit that might be the burial place of the Horseman, there was a voice that was deep and demonic-sounding that said, *"LEAVE—NOW."*

This really surprised me, and when played back several times it sent waves of cold shivers up and down my neck and spine. It definitely sounded like something didn't want

me there. I estimated the voice was recorded just before the
two shadow men appeared.

You have to remember this was back in the 1980s, when
EVP were not as common as they are today with digital
recorders. I had heard stories of UFO researchers who,
while conducting an investigation, picked up voices and
sounds not audible in the room. It happened to me on more
than one occasion.[13] When it happens, you are never prepared for it, so it can scare even the most seasoned paranormal investigator.

A VISIT TO SUNNYSIDE

After an unsettled sleep I awoke early the next morning.
Next on my list was to visit Sunnyside, the estate of Washington Irving in Tarrytown. The house is supposed to be
haunted by the ghost of Irving himself. Local legend says
that Irving loved the home and property so much that when
he died he never left.

I arrived at Sunnyside late in the morning and planned
to take a very close look around not only the house but also
the surrounding property. After arriving I talked with the
estate spokesperson, who informed me that he was unaware
of any ghost sightings. He also added that he spent ten years
walking through the house at all hours of the day and night
and never witnessed anything strange. He did admit to hearing noises that sounded like walking on the upper floor,

---

13. This is documented in a previous book of mine, *Interdimensional
    Universe: The New Science of UFOs, Paranormal Phenomena & Otherdi-
    mensional Beings* (Llewellyn, 2008).

but attributed it to nothing more than an old foundation settling and the wood expanding and contracting with the change of temperature.

I walked into the house, and there was a young woman with her daughter standing at the entrance that led to the living room. The child, who was probably only three years old, was screaming that she did not want to go any farther and was scared. The mother asked the child why she was scared. The child then pointed to a hallway and said there was a man standing there dressed in funny clothes who was telling her to go away.

There was no man in the hall. The child became so upset that the mother had to pick her up and leave the house. Was it possible the little girl saw the ghost of Washington Irving? Young children often see and hear things adults do not. This includes a variety of paranormal phenomena. Perhaps some childhood imaginary friends are not imaginary at all, but real entities that adults cannot see—it really makes you wonder!

My tour through the house was uneventful. I took over twenty-four pictures that day, several in each room in the house. It was time to head back home and place all the information accumulated over the past two days into my files for a permanent record of my investigation into the Legend of Sleepy Hollow.

I once again stopped at the Sleepy Hollow Cemetery to visit Washington Irving's grave and pay my respects. Was the legend of Sleepy Hollow just a story, or was it real? Is it possible that so many people wanted to believe in the legend so badly that their combined subconscious imagination created the apparition? I guess we will never know for sure.

When the pictures of my trip to Sleepy Hollow were finally developed, I quickly scanned through the negatives, but to my dismay there were no ghostly images of the Headless Horseman or Washington Irving.

UPDATE

On June 26, 2010, a fourteen-year-old girl took a picture of an upstairs window while outside the front entrance at Sunnyside. To her surprise, a face was visible in the photo that appears to be Washington Irving himself. The image shows the head and upper body of a man who seems to be holding a quill pen.[14]

---

14. At the time of this writing, this image is available online, at http://www.youtube.com/watch?v=AWm14dok3OA.

CHAPTER 5

THE CURSE
OF THE GREEN WITCH

New England is famous for many things: the Revolutionary War, beautiful fall weather, maple syrup, and of course the celebration of Halloween. However, there is something else New England will also be remembered for, something most residents would like to forget—the infamous witch trials.

The word *witch* in the biblical book of Exodus is a translation of the Hebrew *kashaph*, which itself is derived from the root meaning "to whisper." It does not necessarily mean to speak softly. The meaning of the word in Exodus translates as "one who whispers a spell." The word was also used to identify those who performed secret rituals that were not sanctioned by religious Hebrew law. As far back as 650 BCE, witchcraft was forbidden by Jewish law, since those who practiced it did not follow the Hebrew religion. An individual convicted of practicing witchcraft was stoned to death.[15] In context, the Exodus passage probably was intended to urge Jews to adhere to their own religious practices and not those of surrounding tribes.

Today, the Western world's idea of what a witch should look like conjures up images of an old hag dressed in black wearing a large pointed hat with warts and moles on her face.

The people who were accused of witchcraft in New England in the seventeenth century looked nothing of the sort. Most women and men accused of serving devils were innocent, but some were indeed witches. They were witches in the sense that to some degree they still followed the old Pagan religion of nature worship outlawed by the church in Rome.

During my research, a number of documents were discovered in local archives in Hartford, Connecticut, and Putnam County, New York, indicating the old ways did not completely die out with the emergence of Christianity. It seems the majority of people who still held on to their Pagan beliefs practiced the religion privately. Those who were caught were arrested and often put to death.

The practicing of Pagan beliefs was outlawed by the Roman Catholic Church. This was a deliberate attempt to wipe out other religions in Europe so all people under regulation of the late Roman Empire would become Christians and followers of the church.

---

15. Exodus 22:18: "Thou shalt not suffer a witch to live." Leviticus 20:27: "A man or woman that hath a familiar spirit, or that is a wizard, shall surely be put to death."

The church leaders in Rome were not successful in their attempts to stamp out Paganism, so a disinformation campaign was conceived to associate the old ways with the devil. Even in modern times, many God-fearing Christians still believe the devil exists and is ready to steal their soul should they lose faith. In some cases, fear of the devil is greater than their faith in God.

THE WITCHES OF NEW ENGLAND

When one thinks of the infamous witch trials of New England, Salem, Massachusetts, comes to mind. Although there was a "witch scare" in every New England colony, only two actually put people to death—Massachusetts and Connecticut. Modern residents of the latter state may find this hard to believe, but Connecticut was not immune to the witch-hunt craze of the seventeenth century. Historical documents uncovered prove that the witch hunts *began* in Connecticut.

As in the Massachusetts trials, Connecticut town officials often used "witchcraft" as a means to get rid of undesirable people. Today, the Salem witch trials are considered part of early American history. The state of Massachusetts is very cooperative when releasing records of the trials, but Connecticut is not. Many of the records that document execution, torture, and persecution of innocent people have been conveniently lost, damaged, or misfiled.

In Connecticut in 1647, Alse Young was the first person convicted of being a witch in New England and hanged to death. The evidence against her was conveniently lost after the execution. Even after more than 360 years, the state of

Connecticut still hides in embarrassment at what took place in those early days of colonial America.

STRIKING BACK AT THE DEVIL

According to Connecticut historian Walter Woodward, "In Puritan culture, the devil was a real presence, and residents lived in fear for their souls. For a society that believed the devil is their enemy and who also believed the devil is the strongest power in the universe next to God, when they think they're under attack by the devil, their response is based on a perceived threat. This wasn't just mean-spiritedness. This was the product of intense fear."[16]

If the colonial people of Connecticut thought they were being attacked by the devil, their first response was fear and shock and then the next response would be to strike back. Since they could not attack the devil himself, they went after people whom they thought the demon was working through.

The human psyche really hasn't changed since that time. After the 9/11 attacks, people all across the country were shocked and gripped with fear. The fear was mixed with anger, and Americans were ready to strike out at anyone at whom authorities pointed the finger of guilt. When the names of the terrorists and the cultures and organizations they belonged to were released, Americans were ready to go to war.

---

16. As quoted in Susan Campbell, "Colonial Witch Hysteria Recalled," *Hartford Courant* (Hartford, CT), May 27, 2007.

As with the witch hunts, after 9/11 it was fear and a desire to strike before an attack could take place again that dominated the emotions of the people. There are all sorts of obvious differences between the witch hunts of the seventeenth century and the reaction to 9/11, but the similarity between the two is that, in both cases, a number of innocent people and cultures were singled out and persecuted.

THE CONNECTICUT WITCH TRIALS

Although all the proceedings were probably well documented, many of the trial records no longer exist. Of those documents that did survive, it appears the process that led to a witch trial began with a formal complaint. A single witness was all it took to support a witchcraft conviction in Connecticut before 1662. The magistrate would then gather information and depositions prior to the arrest. When enough evidence was obtained, the alleged witch was arrested and placed in a holding cell that was more like a dungeon. The case would then be scheduled for a court date.

During my research, no information or documents were found to indicate the accused in Connecticut were represented by counsel. I made several phone calls to local historians and Connecticut's legal information office, but no one seemed to know the answer. I do know for sure that people tried for witchcraft in Salem were not given counsel. It was most likely the same in Connecticut, since just the accusation of witchcraft and dealing with the devil made people look at the accused as some type of evil subhuman who had no rights as a human being.

There was a total of forty-one witch trials in Connecticut between 1647 and 1697. Fourteen of these people were definitely executed, and five more could have been, but no one knows for sure since the records are incomplete. It is most likely that the additional five were executed, since there was a conviction. This would bring the total to nineteen, which is coincidentally the same number as the Salem witch executions.

I found a court transcript regarding the statement of Rebecca Greensmith, who was tried for witchcraft along with her husband Nathanial in Hartford during the summer of 1662. This was an amazing discovery, because it is the only statement made by a defendant that survived to this day. It does indicate that unlike the Salem trials, the accused in Connecticut, although also denied counsel, were allowed to make a statement in defense of the charges against them.[17] However, it seems that Rebecca Greensmith's plea to the court was in vain, as she and her husband were hanged in 1662.

The Salem trials were partially vindictive in nature, but the Connecticut witch trials were different. They were controlled by a fear of evil so terrible that it made neighbors turn on each other. People were afraid to speak of controversial things, always attended Sunday mass, and kept the Sabbath day sacred for fear of also being accused of witchcraft.

---

17. Source: Connecticut Judicial Branch, Law Libraries archives, Court proceedings dated 1640–1700: Document 1622-8-23-62, Hartford, Connecticut.

After spending days going through old documents in Hartford, it was clear to me that some of the accused witches were Pagans. They stayed true to the old religion that had existed in Europe before Christianity. Today we call this "old religion" Wicca. Yes, it seems that several of the women and men were indeed "witches," but they were not evil or servants of the devil; they were nature worshippers.

Three of the accused were often reported collecting green plants and flowers and placing them on a small altar in their home. It was also noticed they honored the old Pagan holidays.

My investigation centered on one particular individual who was tried and hanged in Connecticut as a witch. In order to get the information required, considerable research had to be done on the witch trials in Connecticut. This was important, because the woman who was the focus of my investigation was Goodwife (Lucinda) Knapp.

Goodwife was not her first name, but rather a polite way to address a married woman in the seventeenth century. It was often shortened to "Goody." In more modern times, Goodwife or Goody was replaced by the title of *Mrs.* Women with a higher status in society were referred to as *Mistress*.

In the way she was executed and buried, Goodwife Knapp was treated differently from the other so-called witches who were put to death during that time. Her trial and execution were so unique that it required years of research to find out why. When the answer to this mystery was finally discovered, it would lead me on an adventure into the dark history of Connecticut, to a shadowy secret that began during colonial times and was kept well hidden.

SEARCHING FOR THE GREEN WITCH

Roger Knapp was born in England sometime around 1618. Mr. Knapp came to New England in the early 1640s. In 1644 he settled in Fairfield, which at that time was known as the colony of New Haven. Not much is known about Roger Knapp except that he is listed as a farmer and an Indian trader.

His wife, who was considerably younger, was known only as "Goodwife" Knapp. There is very little historical information about where she originally came from, and there is only one sentence that appears in the trial record that indicated she often openly talked about the old Pagan ways. The colonial people of seventeenth-century Connecticut believed one who acknowledged the "old ways" must be in league with the devil, since the church had outlawed this practice many years before.

Knapp liked to collect green ferns and place them around her property and at certain places in town, apparently honoring a number of Pagan festivals. She was given the name "Green Witch" sometime after her execution.

A DARK TIME IN AMERICAN HISTORY

Goodwife Knapp was accused during a time when the witch trials and executions were at their peak in the British Isles. When people from England and Scotland migrated to the colonies, they brought their fears and superstitions with them.

Typically, the witch was accused of associating with the devil and using her powers and spells to attack people who crossed her. The "evidence" was usually a series of unusual happenings that occurred in the presence of the accused or strange behavior that was deemed to be inappropriate for that time.

The court accepted statements of witnesses who claimed they, a member of their family, or even an animal they owned was harmed by the spells cast by the alleged witch. In many cases, the accused women seem to have been more outspoken than others. A woman speaking her mind during colonial America was not tolerated by the village men.

There is enough circumstantial evidence to indicate Goodwife Knapp was indeed a follower of the old Celtic religion. The problem was that when Knapp came to the New World, she openly talked about her beliefs. This made her a target from the first day she arrived in the New Haven Colony.

It seems people were very leery and almost afraid of her, because she openly discussed and celebrated certain Pagan festivals and holidays. The men in the New Haven Colony would insult her by calling her "simple-minded." In the seventeenth century this was a polite way of calling someone stupid or crazy. *Simple-minded* was also often used to describe someone who made fantastic claims or had ideas that did not fit in with the normal behavior of society. Today, if a person claims he or she was abducted by aliens, most people would respond by saying they were crazy. In the seventeenth century they would be called "simple-minded."

Goodwife Knapp was referred to as "simple-minded" by her accusers because she did not fit in or behave like the other women of the colony. Apparently, this was evidence enough to arrest her. The witch hunters of the village claimed she was working with Satan to corrupt the other women of the colony with "simple-minded" ideas.

MORE EVIDENCE

In October 2010 I found a document while exploring the computer-based historical archives of the Peabody Museum at Yale University in New Haven. This document, in my opinion, provides evidence that Goodwife Knapp may have indeed been a follower of what we call Wicca today. The document is a statement from a woman in the New Haven Colony and was admitted as evidence at the Knapp trial. It clearly presents information that Knapp collected crystals from local Indians and believed they had magical powers:

> Hester, Wife of Andrew Ward, testified, "that aboute a Day after that Goodwife Knapp was condemned for a Witch, she goeing to the Prison House where said Knapp was kept, she, the said Knapp, voluntarily . . . told her an Indian brought unto her two little Things brighter than the light of the Day [crystals], and told the said Goodwife Staplyes they were Indian Gods, as the Indian called them, and the Indian withall told her, the said Staplyes, if she would keepe them, she should be so big Rich, all one God; and that the said Staplyes told the

said Knapp she gave them again to the said Indian, but she could not tell whether she did so or no.

In the seventeenth century, the so-called Indian gods were thought to be Satan himself. The people of the New Haven Colony considered the local Native Americans to be pagans and believed they were misled by Satan through no fault of their own. Ministers of the Connecticut colonies tried to convert Native Americans to Christianity. In some cases they were successful, but in most they failed. Native American medicine, rattles, crystals, and other things used in ceremonies were considered instruments of the devil and his minions.

A QUICK TRIAL, EXECUTION, AND BURIAL

During the witch trials the magistrate would look for evidence that the accused witch harmed someone in the community by conjuring a spell, demon, or specter. The accuser would also have to provide testimony saying they saw the accused do magical things like flying on a pole or changing into an animal. In the case of Goodwife Knapp there was no evidence of this nature against her and very little testimony. It's clear from the surviving documents that people in the colony wanted to get rid of her. One sure way to accomplish this during those dark days was to claim someone was a witch.

The trial and execution of Goodwife Knapp was one of the most noteworthy of all the witch trials in the state of Connecticut. From the material I've read, she was without a doubt a pleasant young woman who went out of her way to help people. According to recent findings, Knapp was very attractive with a wonderful, gentle personality.

Since she was so friendly and physically attractive, Goodwife Knapp may have been considered a threat by the other women of the New Haven Colony. Recent court documents obtained at the archives of the Hartford judicial library indicate the magistrate's court considered Knapp a woman of "good repute, not argumentative, or an outcast, and she did not have a vile mouth."

Since Goodwife Knapp was "different" from the rest of the women around her, she was singled out and under suspicion. That was enough to set the villagers with talk of witchcraft, gossip, and scandal about the unfortunate woman, which led to her death.

Pending her trial, Goodwife Knapp was committed to the house of correction, or common jail for the safekeeping of criminals. One can only imagine what terrors of mind and spirit this gentle, beautiful, nature-loving, "simple-minded" young woman must have endured. Her place of captivity was cold, gloomy, comfortless, and unsanitary. The dungeon was constructed of rotting logs and stones, with a single window blocked by iron bars and a massive door.

The trial of Goodwife Knapp was quick, and she was sentenced to death by hanging. From the day she was accused until her execution at Try's Field in what is now Fairfield, her accusers threatened Knapp with physical harm in an attempt to make her confess to consorting with the devil and his demons.

Six women and one man brought the only evidence against her. These were the women whose husbands at one time commented on how beautiful and pleasant Goodwife Knapp was. The women claimed that Knapp put a spell on their husbands with the purpose of seducing them so they would feel obligated to serve the devil.

Of the women, a Mistress Pell, seems to have been the chief spokeswoman, and each member of the committee served in some degree as an inquisitor. They baited, badgered, and warned Knapp that unless she confessed she would be tortured. Despite being threatened, Goodwife Knapp insisted she was innocent and denied the charges made against her. During her trial, she told one of her accusers, "Take heed the devil have not a hold on you and that I am innocent."

Throughout the arrest, trial, conviction, and execution of Goodwife Knapp there is no word of her husband, Roger, coming to her aid. Fairfield folklore has it that he fled the colony since he feared he would be implicated himself.

The day Goodwife Knapp was buried, many of the local residents felt that she should not be in the same cemetery as their relatives, who were "God-fearing" people and members of the church in good standing. One night her grave was desecrated and the body partially exhumed. However, it seems whoever was responsible did not finish the horrible act and fled before the break of dawn. When the condition of the gravesite was discovered, all kinds of rumors quickly spread throughout the colony.

One story that spread like wildfire was that Satan brought her back to life. During the night she struggled to get out of the grave and once again died at sunrise. Many people of the colony actually believed when the sun once again set, Goodwife Knapp would come to life and seek revenge.

The less superstitious and more educated people of the colony had a different theory. They believed that a group of men tried to exhume the body of Knapp, since they were appalled that she was buried next to their family members. Their plan was to take the body and bury it in an undisclosed location. Another theory states several men who condemned her wanted to dig up her body and look for witch marks (moles) so they could feel more justified with what they had done.

Although the individuals who were suspected of doing the dastardly deed never confessed, a document still exists at the Peabody Museum that indicts them. There was never any proof of wrongdoing, so the matter was dropped.

A local minister, Reverend John Davenport, when asked about the grave, told his parish that he was sure Satan was going to resurrect Goodwife Knapp from the dead to feed off the living during the night and get her revenge on those who had testified against her. The minister's sermon created a wave of fear. The people of the colony demanded her body be taken out of the grave and reburied far from the village.

After considerable debate, the governing board of the town and magistrate ruled the body should be exhumed and taken to another place to be buried. This place would be kept secret. For over 350 years, the location of the body of the Green Witch remained hidden, but apparently not to all.

THE SECRET BURIAL PLACE

My investigation took me from Fairfield to New Haven, then to Hartford, and finally to Redding, Connecticut. According to records and hearsay, the Green Witch was buried in a small plot of land in a wooded area in Redding. There is no document of a witch trial in that town, and the burial places of all the other alleged witches are accounted for.

I found one small handwritten document at the Redding-Georgetown town hall archives that indicated that a body of a woman put to death as a witch was brought in from another colony and buried in Redding. Using the process of elimination, this had to be the resting place of the Green Witch.

A number of years ago I was a consultant to police in Connecticut. They would call me if a crime had an occult connection. If symbols or artifacts were found in a crime scene, I was contacted with the hope that I could shed some light on the case.

One day in 1986, while at the Norwalk, Connecticut, police headquarters on a UFO case, I had a conversation with a state police officer. He asked me where I was from, and I answered Bethel. He replied, half laughing, "Oh, Bethel. That's right next to Redding—*Devil Worship USA!*"

His comment caught me off guard. I knew Redding was a strange place, but I was actually quite surprised when the officer began to tell me about occult-related crimes they were investigating in that town. The possibility that Good-wife Knapp was buried in Redding is almost poetic justice, since this small Connecticut town has a history of paranormal happenings. If she was indeed a witch practicing black magic, then Knapp would have felt right at home in this small New England town.

A MODERN-DAY FOLLOWING

Through my many contacts and interaction with occult groups in New England, I discovered that today a number of cults exist in Connecticut whose members believe the legend of the Green Witch is fact and not fiction. I found this strange. Is it possible that Goodwife Knapp had a following when she was alive, and those people slowly and secretly evolved into a cult that survived into modern times?

Initially, efforts to track down this group proved to be in vain since they were very secretive. I did discover, mostly from hearsay, that the group had thirteen leaders who were very prominent citizens of the communities of Fairfield, New Haven, Redding, Georgetown, Weston, Bethel, and Greenwich, Connecticut. Each of the thirteen cult leaders, all women, call themselves a *High Priestess* and have twelve apprentices under them.

Eventually, through my many connections with the police and local occult groups, I was able to discover the name of a High Priestess who was in charge of the group in Greenwich. It is not possible for me to name her since there is no documented proof. Also, this person is the matron of a very influential family in that town, and at this time it would not be a good idea to single her out. In the past after exposing quite a number of occult groups, I was often stalked and threatened with death. I'm sure my readers can understand why this information is being withheld.

THE CURSE

My investigation to track down the legend of the Green Witch seemed to have hit a brick wall. Then, in the summer of 1991, I got a break. As a result of my asking around, I was contacted by a young woman who claimed to have once been a member of a cult in Connecticut that focuses on the witches who were executed in colonial times. The cult's belief is centered on the Green Witch. My contact, who prefers not to be named for fear of reprisals, claimed the cult leaders and the followers believe in the legend and the curse. She told me the cult members actually believed Knapp was a powerful witch who practiced black magic. I then asked what she meant about a curse. Although my contact did not know the details, she repeated to me what she heard from the High Priestess during her initiation into the cult.

Although there is no historical documentation to prove the claims of my contact, it appears from what I have been told that the people in her cult believe it. The former members of this most secretive group in New England call themselves "Disciples of the Green Witch." They believe that as Goodwife Knapp was taken to the gallows, she placed a curse on the people who persecuted her and their descendants. She told them that one day she would rise from the grave and get her revenge. Although there is some documentation

that moments before Knapp was hanged she tried to impli-
cate others as being witches, there is no written account of
a curse.

The story of the curse is quite interesting, since it sounds
like a plot for a Hollywood horror movie. It seems that after
the Green Witch was hanged, her body was placed in a grave
in the local cemetery. The legend says she came back to life
and tried to leave the grave. At her first attempt she was
partially unsuccessful and once again died at sunrise. Believing she would rise again at sunset, the townspeople took
her body to a plot of land far from the colony (Redding) and
buried it in an unmarked grave. A minister whose name
is unknown placed a curse on Knapp after she was buried,
trapping her spirit within the confines of the grave.

Her modern-day followers believe that one day (if they
have not done so already) they will be able to break the
curse and the spirit of the Green Witch will be free. She
will then enter the body of a young woman brought to the
gravesite and live again. The cult members also believe that
if they help the Green Witch get her revenge, she will share
her secrets of magic with the leaders of the group.

My contact had no idea where the Green Witch was buried. She told me this information was restricted to the "elder
members" of the cult. This so-called curse is not backed up
by any type of historical record; it seems to be faith that is
the driving force for this group. The entire tale may have
been made up and used by the cult leaders to keep the cult
together and control its members and give them purpose.

BACK ON THE TRAIL OF THE GREEN WITCH

After looking over hundreds of historical records of births and deaths in the town of Redding, my quest to find the grave of the Green Witch led me to a small cemetery on the outskirts of town. From the land documents I uncovered, it appears that this small graveyard was once just a parcel of land owned by the Davenport family (and their descendants) of the New Haven Colony. Sometime in the late eighteenth century it became a family cemetery. Today, no one seems to know who owns the small parcel of land, and a search through public records was in vain.

It was difficult at first to find, since it was located off a side road that was rarely traveled. After driving around for an hour I finally found the cemetery and arrived late in the afternoon on October 31, 1993. I was a little concerned, since there was one house across the street that had a clear view of the cemetery.

Being brought up to be respectful of the property of others, I went up to and knocked on the door of the house. After all, if this was a family plot it would have been wrong to simply trespass without permission.

The owner of the home answered, a man perhaps in his mid-thirties. He said he really didn't know who owned the cemetery, and to his knowledge no one in over one hundred years had been buried there. The gentleman, whose name was David, asked what my interest was. My reply was quick and simple, that I investigate reports of the paranormal and was now researching the witch trials of Connecticut. I also mentioned it was possible one of the witches put to death was buried in the lot across the street. David's face went pale. He then said, "Have I got a story for you! Please come in." After a quick cup of coffee David began his strange tale:

"It was last year on Halloween Eve. I live alone and really don't get any trick-or-treaters, so I leave the light off. I think most of the families that live around here have heard that the old cemetery is haunted. It's most likely because of this that the kids are afraid to walk around here at night, especially on Halloween. I never gave any credibility to the stories about ghosts, but after that night last year it made me consider they may be true.

"It was about 11 p.m. on October 30th. I looked out the front window and saw a number of lights moving around in the cemetery. At first they looked like lanterns, and then I realized the lights began to rise upward, apparently higher than a person can reach. The lights appeared to slowly drift over to the left side of the cemetery where there are no gravestones. I thought about calling the police but didn't, since they most likely had enough to do around Halloween.

"I walked out my front door and began to cross the street. It was then that I saw the outline of a number of dark figures holding what appeared to be old-fashioned lanterns with candles in them. They were wearing robes; they looked like monks. They were all circling a tree, chanting something in a language I couldn't understand. When I called out to them and said hello they froze in their tracks. There was a feeling of evil, anger, and something else that's indescribable. It was then that I backed off and quickly went back to my house and called the police.

"To make a long story short, the police came within a half hour and found nothing. Since that experience, every once in a while I would look over to the cemetery and see a light floating around and then disappearing."

After several questions I thanked David for his report and proceeded across the street to the cemetery. It was now about four in the afternoon and the sun was beginning to set. The gravestones had an unusual fog around them that made the cemetery look even spookier. The place had a very eerie feel to it, and there was definitely some type of heavy energy surrounding the property.

As I walked through the rusted metal gate a feeling of depression seemed to grasp my soul. If people do leave a psychic signature after they pass over, then this place and the people buried here must have had a traumatic life. Then the thought came to me—perhaps I was picking up the presence of the Green Witch, whose soul is still trapped in the grave.

According to the legend, the grave was unmarked but near a tree. I walked around looking at the stones, and although most of them were weathered away some of the names of those buried could still be read. I looked around at the headstones and then saw an extremely worn stone that read *Davenport*. It was now clear I was in the right place.

I walked to an isolated part of the cemetery and saw a tree that was out in the open with no other gravestones around it. Near the tree was a depression, as if the ground was slowly caving in. From my experience at Sleepy Hollow I knew this was an unmarked grave. Did I find the gravesite of the Green Witch? I firmly believed I did; it had to be!

The sun was setting and it was getting dark, so I left. My plan was to return the next day, on November first, but earlier in the day to take pictures. I also wanted to spend more time looking over the rest of the land.

THE BLACK CANDLES

The next day I arrived early in the morning and walked over to what I thought was the unmarked grave. I was surprised to see six black, round candles surrounding the depression in the ground. It looked like someone had been performing an all-night ritual, since the candles were not there the day before and were half-exhausted. My thoughts reflected back to David's sightings of the hooded people around the grave. Could they have been the modern-day followers of the Green Witch? Was it possible they were at the gravesite last night on Halloween to perform a ritual?

I thought about the story of the curse that trapped the Green Witch in her grave and the legend of her resurrection. Was it possible her followers were attempting to free the trapped spirit? In the days and months to follow I returned to the gravesite several times, but nothing unusual was noticed. My next plan was to wait until the following year's Halloween, at which time I would do an all-night stakeout.

HALLOWEEN STAKEOUT

On Halloween night in 1994 I returned to the graveyard at sundown and parked up the road and out of sight. It was my intention not to attract attention or scare anyone away. As the sun set and night fell, the air temperature cooled down considerably. I didn't want to bring attention to myself by running the engine, so I tolerated the cold.

At 11 p.m. I got out of the car and walked to the entrance of the cemetery. I approached the suspected gravesite. Nothing. I went back to the car and actually fell asleep for three hours.

During that period of sleep I had lucid dreams about colonial America and the trial and sentence of Goodwife Knapp. During the hanging I awoke with jolt. It was very real, as though I had traveled back into time to witness the terrible event. The interesting thing was that I appeared to be just a spectator; nobody seemed to hear or see me.

The dashboard clock in the car read 2:23 a.m. I got out of the car feeling rather light-headed and walked to the gravesite. I was shocked to see seven black candles surrounding the pit. The wicks were still slightly warm and the wax somewhat soft. Whoever did this had been there within the last twenty minutes and left. I just missed them! I looked around for another hour, but found no one responsible. Puzzled, and amazed at what was found, I returned to my car and left for home.

During the next several nights my visits to the old cemetery turned up nothing. It seems that I would have to wait a year to try and catch the person or group who set out the black candles. Due to personal obligations and a list of problems that plagued me for the next six years, I was not able to return to the graveyard on Halloween until the year 2000. The time period from 1994 to 2000 was a rough time for me. Everything seemed to go wrong. It was if someone or something placed a curse or spell on me to keep me busy and divert my attention away from discovering the secret of the Green Witch.

HALLOWEEN 2000

This time an old friend named Tom joined me. Tom shared my interest in the pursuit of the paranormal and would occasionally join me on one of my night-stalking adventures. We arrived at one in the morning and I once again parked my car on the hill, no farther than one hundred feet from the cemetery entrance.

At two in the morning we entered the cemetery, walked over to the gravesite, and found nothing unusual. Tom wanted to go back to the car, but I suggested we go behind a nearby wall and wait to see if someone or something appeared.

After a one-hour wait nothing happened. Tom was elderly with arthritis and complained of being cold and in pain. We decided our vigil was a waste of time and walked back to the car. I turned over the engine and put on the heat. We sat there for about thirty seconds when Tom said he'd left his flashlight in the cemetery.

I grabbed my own flashlight and ran in, passing the gravesite of the Green Witch. I had a very strong feeling of being watched; it felt very unpleasant. Tom was calling from the car asking if everything was all right, since I was taking a long time to return.

After returning to the car I told Tom what I felt. He replied, "Yes, I feel it, too. We should get out of here. This is not right." I wanted to stay and solve the mystery of the black candles once and for all, but Tom was tired and not feeling well so I drove him home. He lived only about twenty minutes from the cemetery, so I decided to go back after I dropped him off and check on the gravesite. When I arrived I was shocked to see six black candles surrounding the grave and one white one at its head (or foot). The wax was still a little soft and one of the wicks was warm. I had just missed whoever was responsible. I then took a number of pictures and went home.

Four days later while driving home from work, I stopped by the old cemetery and noticed the candles were gone. If the person or people responsible did not remove them, then someone was taking care of the property.

I am sorry to say that Tom never returned with me to try and solve the mystery, since he passed on just over a year later. His death was the result of a hit-and-run while he was walking his dog only several hundred feet from his home in Danbury.

Over the next two years I once again staked out the gravesite, but witnessed nothing unusual. It has been a number of years since my last visit. I plan to go once again next Halloween night to see if the candles appear again. Perhaps one day I will catch the person or people lighting them.

Were they followers of the cult of the Green Witch? Whoever they were, they seemed to have the same information I had about her resting place. Perhaps the reason the candles were never seen again is because the curse was broken. Did her soul finally find peace on the other side, or is she now in a new body, stalking the descendants of the colonists who persecuted her more than 350 years ago?

CHAPTER 6

EXTRAORDINARY MANIFESTATIONS

Over the years I have received many calls from people re-
porting all kinds of paranormal experiences. One of the most
frequently reported are manifestations that are religious in
nature. In the majority of these cases, the individual inter-
prets the apparition as being a religious figure, especially if
they have a Catholic background. The witness seems more
comfortable when dealing with this type of extraordinary experience if they convince themselves the "vision" was sent
by God.

Although in cases like this there are very few hoaxes,
most of the so-called apparitions of religious figures are
explainable or the result of someone who is trying to escape
a troubled life. However, if the person wants to see Jesus,
an angel, or the Virgin Mary, then no amount of proof will
convince them otherwise.

In many of these cases the witness feels the manifestation was meant just for them and they were chosen by God. They want to believe they have been singled out; they want to believe there is a higher power looking over them—but the bottom line is they want to believe too much.

THE BEING IN THE PURPLE ROBE

On July 19, 2004, I was contacted by an individual named Jake, who then resided in Toms River, New Jersey. Jake was in his mid-thirties at the time. He claimed that on several occasions a tall being with long black hair and beard, dressed in a flowing purple robe, appeared in his bedroom at two or three in the morning. Jake also said that the last time the entity appeared, it vanished with a burst of light and "burned" an image of itself on his bedroom wall.

Physical evidence of any kind following a paranormal experience is very rare, so I decided to drive down to his home to see for myself and get the rest of his story firsthand.

I arrived on Saturday, and Jake invited me in to his home. We walked into the living room and sat down. I asked to see the image on the wall. Jake replied, "Before I show you the image, let me tell you the story behind it." He then told me he believed the person in the purple robe was really Jesus. He believed that Jesus had specially selected him to become a prophet.

When I heard this, a red flag went up in my mind and I began to think this just might be a wild goose chase. I asked Jake if the being told him directly that he was Jesus.

Jake replied he did not, but the being appeared exactly as he envisioned Jesus would look like. Jake then began his story, which appears below in his own words.

JAKE'S ENCOUNTER

"I was up late at night with a headache and didn't feel well. There was a feeling someone was in the house with me. I live alone, and other than my mother, who lives in Connecticut, I have no family. So the feeling was that who or whatever was in the house with me I had to face alone.

"I went to bed. At perhaps two or three in the morning a voice told me to wake up and open my eyes. I could not move my body. I was able to angle my head and eyes to look at the foot of the bed. There I saw a man about six feet tall enter my room. He was floating, made no noise, and was dressed in a long loose-fitting robe that was purple in color. He had long, jet-black, shoulder-length hair with a long beard. There was a white glow around him, which I saw reflect off the television set. Then there was this flash of light, and the next thing I remember this man is alongside the bed next to my right hand. He was looking directly at me. His eyes were black and they sparkled. In my mind I asked if he was Jesus. He smiled and nodded his head to say yes. Then there was a flash of light and he vanished. I closed my eyes and experienced the most peaceful sleep in my life.

"The next night at the same time Jesus came back, but this time he remained at the foot of the bed. A flood of thoughts then came into my mind. I don't remember them all, but some were about things that were going to happen, like the end of the world was coming very soon. He wanted me to take this information and tell everyone that the second coming was going to happen soon and we should all prepare. Then he vanished in a flash of light so bright it burned an image on my wall."

I had a great number of questions to ask Jake, since the two incidents had taken place less than a week previously and were still fresh in his mind. I asked once again to see the image on the wall in the bedroom. I followed Jake upstairs and into the room. As we walked I noticed nothing on the walls until Jake pointed it out to me.

There was a very faint image on the wall, and unless someone pointed it out to you it would hardly be noticed. With considerable imagination the shape of a person might be made out, but it was extremely vague. Jake insisted it was an image of Jesus on his wall and "the Lord" left it for him to prove to others that he witnessed a miracle.

I have to say the image on the wall was inconclusive, and it wasn't evidence enough to support Jake's amazing claim. He then took his finger and pointed out a beard, face, eyes, hair, nose, and even the outline of the robes the entity was wearing. I did not see any of this and left somewhat disappointed.

CONCLUSIONS

Was it possible that Jake saw something on the wall that I did not? It was my opinion that he was telling the truth, or the truth as he wanted to believe it. The experience of his nighttime encounter with the being in the purple robe was most likely a real event. It is possible the entity identified itself as Jesus to gain his confidence and subdue his fear. It is interesting to note the entity appeared to Jake exactly like he thought Jesus would look. This is a common theme in encounters of this nature. The entity will take on a shape that is familiar or pleasing to the person so they will accept whatever is about to take place.

Jake continued to have nighttime visitations. He called me for the last time in 2007 and said, "God had chosen me to be a prophet to herald the second coming of Christ." Jake then told me that he had quit his job and was moving out to a desert to fast and prepare his body and soul. As of the writing of this book, I have not been able to reach him. His phone is disconnected, and mail was returned with no forwarding address.

APPARITIONS, APPARITIONS EVERYWHERE

Since 1982 I have been called on many an occasion to view alleged images of Mary and Jesus in bathtubs, broken trees, window panes, subway walls, and a host of other places too numerous to name. In my opinion, the images looked nothing like the religious figures mentioned. Yet the person who discovered it or on whose property the image appeared insists they can clearly see a face and body. In all of the cases investigated by me, the people had a deep-rooted religious belief and almost all of them were raised Roman Catholic.

A COMMON THEME

Of all the religious images that appear, apparitions of the Virgin Mary are the most common. In the twentieth century there were over four hundred reports in which the faithful saw her image appear in one form or another. Two hundred of these reports were made in a period from 1993 until 1999. In some rare cases the apparition was accompanied by other forms of phenomena. These include glowing disks in the sky, unusual lights appearing around the manifestation, and, on occasion, angelic-like beings complete with wings and halo.

The most well-documented apparitions of the twentieth century took place in Portugal, Belgium, Japan, Italy, Venezuela, Rwanda, and Egypt. These manifestations were images of the Virgin Mary that appeared on walls, trees, rocks, and even in mashed potatoes.

In most of these cases, the image is shadowy and undefined. The most interesting of this type of phenomenon is when the entity appears as a glowing, angelic-like being. These are called "Marian apparitions" by the Roman Catholic Church.

HISTORICALLY NOTEWORTHY MARIAN APPARITIONS

Sometime around 1295 in Oxford, England, a Franciscan priest was defending the Immaculate Conception against the Dominicans when a glowing image of the Virgin Mary appeared on the wall. Soon after, in honor of the miracle manifestation, the Feast of the Immaculate Conception was declared to be a universal holy day of obligation.

In 1830, a young nun in Paris named Catherine Labouré began having Marian visitations. She claimed that an angel in white led her to the convent chapel late at night, where she saw, spoke with, and touched the Virgin Mary. Later in the year, the Lady appeared once again, dressed in white, and stood in the chapel with a serpent beneath her feet. The apparition was surrounded by an oval flame that framed the words *Mary, conceived without sin, pray for us, who have recourse to you.*

A voice instructed Catherine to have a medal struck showing the vision. She was told by the apparition that whoever wears it will receive grace from God and protection from evil.

In 1842 in La Salette, France, an eleven-year-old boy and a fourteen-year-old girl heard a thunderous sound and then saw a flash of light from which a lady appeared, dressed in white and gold, with a cap of roses on her head. She was surrounded by a brilliant light and was crying. The lady told the children that Sunday was being desecrated, and the peasants were blaspheming the church with foul language. She went on to say if there was no change, there would be great disasters, the harvest would fail, and people would starve. The lady told the children she could no longer keep God from inflicting punishment.

The local parish priest declared the Lady to be the Blessed Virgin; the apparitions were later approved by the Bishop of Grenoble, and pilgrimages began to the location where the children had their vision. The young girl later became a nun and continued to receive visions and revelations.

In 1858, a series of visions took place that would result in the establishment of the most famous of Marian shrines. At the grotto of Massabielle at Lourdes, fourteen-year-old Bernadette Soubirous saw "a glowing white light in the shape of a woman." Under questioning by the town priest, she elaborated that the "Lady" was a pretty young girl in a white dress and veil, "with a blue sash and a yellow rose on each foot." She said the vision most resembled a statue of the Blessed Virgin in the parish church. Bernadette said the Lady was not a statue, but alive.

The Lady, who carried a rosary over her arm, spoke in the local dialect, in a very polite manner, and called for penance. Bernadette was given three "secrets," and asked to pray for the conversion of sinners.

The apparition asked for a procession and for a chapel to be built on the site. Bernadette was instructed to dig for a spring that would usher waters with great healing powers. This spring was already known to exist, but never dug and made into a well. People who came and drank from the waters of the well claimed to be miraculously healed of many ailments, including terminal diseases.

Over the next several weeks Bernadette would recite the rosary and go into trances. The Lady announced her name as *"I am the Virgin of the Immaculate Conception."* During the following October, the ecclesiastical authorities took charge, and they confirmed the apparition was of the Blessed Virgin. As a result of this validation, the shrine of Our Lady of

Lourdes was authorized, and plans were made for the construction of a chapel and sanctuary. In 1933 Bernadette was canonized by the Catholic Church as a saint.

In August 1879, fifteen people aged from six to seventy-five years old saw an apparition at the parish church at Knock, Ireland. The vision was in the form of an altar on which the Virgin Mary stood with a crown on her head made of stars. There were also two other figures that were identified as Saint Joseph and Saint John the Evangelist, who was dressed as a bishop and apparently preaching. During the apparition, witnesses reported that several angels appeared out of circles in the sky and hovered above the altar.

The figures and the altar were about two feet above the ground. They were motionless, except that from time to time they moved to the front or back of the altar. No word was spoken to any of the hundreds of people who witnessed the event.

A shrine was eventually built in anticipation of huge numbers of pilgrims, but somehow the shrine never achieved great popularity. In 1954 Pope Pius XII blessed the Knock shrine at St. Peter's and gave permission for it to be called *Our Lady of Knock*.

In 1917, at Cova da Iria, near the village of Fátima in Portugal, the most famous of the Marian apparitions of the twentieth century took place. Three children—Lucia, age ten; Francisco, age nine; and Jacinta, age seven—saw flashes that looked like "lightning" near the ground. Immediately after they saw the light, there was a sound like thunder and a "pretty young Lady" appeared near a tree, who told the children she came from Heaven.

The children were told to come to the same spot on the thirteenth day of the month for the next six months, and the purpose of the vision would be revealed. The apparition told the children a little friend of theirs who had recently died was in Heaven, but another was in Purgatory "till the end of the world."

At first, the boy Francisco could not see the vision and never heard "the Lady" speak. Jacinta both saw and heard, but never spoke to the Lady. It seemed that Lucia was the focus of communication at the time. On other occasions they were told to say the rosary and pray especially to be "saved from the fires of Hell." Lucia was told "secrets" and saw a terrifying vision of the future. The Lady promised to return and perform a miracle on October 13th so that all would believe.

When Lucia told her mother about the vision, she was punished for telling lies. When the story of their encounter spread throughout town, the children were questioned by a local atheist administrator. He interrogated the children and imprisoned them for two days, but they stuck to their story.

October 13th was a day of high winds and pouring rain. A crowd of seventy thousand people assembled at the site of the apparition, expecting a miracle. According to the statement of Father John, a Roman Catholic priest, everyone was highly excited—kneeling, praying, and asking for a sign and miracle from God.

The Lady appeared but was seen only by the children. The Lady told the children she was the Lady of the Rosary (Virgin Mary) and that the war (World War I) would end that day. The prophecy was incorrect, since the war did not end until thirteen months later. It is, however, interesting to note that the manifestation occurred on the thirteenth, and the war did in fact end thirteen months later.

The apparition then disappeared, and the famous "miracle of the sun" took place. The rain and high winds stopped and all was calm. Lucia cried out, "Look at the sun!" The crowd looked up to see the sun spinning in circles and emitting colored rays of light. The sun then zigzagged from east to west and apparently seemed to fall toward Earth, making the crowd fear that it was the end of the world. As the crowd screamed and covered their heads, the sun returned to its place in the sky. What was unexplainable is the "miracle" was not seen by everyone in the crowd. To this day, not one of the so-called miracles at Fátima has been confirmed with supporting information.

Lucia became a nun, and continued to have visions and revelations. In 1925 the Lady appeared to her with the baby Jesus in her arms. The following year, the infant Jesus appeared alone to Lucia. Then, in 1929, the Lady told Lucia that in Russia there was a plan to take peace away from the Earth and start a great war that would lead to the destruction of the world.

Lucia wrote a detailed account of the apparitions, which included previous appearances of an "angel" to the children. According to Lucia, in 1915 the angel, who identified himself as the "angel of peace," had appeared to them "like a person wrapped in a white sheet." He appeared to be a youth of fifteen years, "with skin whiter than snow."

In 1941 and 1942 Lucia revealed still more visions and was shown a terrifying vision of Hell with red fire, black demons, screams of pain, and Satan himself. In 1960 the Second Vatican Council officially recognized the apparitions as *Our Lady of Fátima*.

Between 1961 and 1965 in Garabandal, Spain, a series of apparitions took place to pre-teen girls. The girls claimed to have witnessed ten appearances of the Virgin Mary and the Archangel Michael.

On June 18, 1961, while playing in a park, they saw a flash of light and heard a "thunderous sound." They looked, and out of the light came the Archangel Michael. The girls described him as a young boy dressed in blue with rose-colored wings, pale white skin, and dark eyes.

The following month, with hundreds of witnesses present, the girls went into a two-hour trance and gave messages to the crowd from the angel. The next day, during another trance, the children claimed they saw the Virgin Mary in white and blue, with a crown of stars on her head. Sometimes she appeared with the baby Jesus, which the girls said on one occasion they were allowed to hold. The trances lasted from a few minutes to three hours. While in trance the girls would hand the Virgin Mary (apparition) objects such as rosaries, medals, and crucifixes to bless for the hundreds of pilgrims who attended.

Although no one in the crowd said they saw or heard anything, later several people who were present during one of the trances came forward to testify they saw a wafer appear on the tongue of one of the girls when she claimed the "Archangel Michael" was giving her Communion.

The messages from the apparition contained warnings of great punishments, which could only be averted by many sacrifices and penances.

A young Jesuit priest present at the time claimed he also saw the miraculous vision and said it was the happiest day of his life. He then told everyone the apparition told him he was going to Heaven. He died the next day. Some people present claimed later to have seen the sun "dance," and a red star with a tail appear in the sky. During one visitation the girls said the apparition came in a mysterious cloud of "fire."

From 1968 until 1971, apparitional appearances over the Coptic church of Saint Mary in Zeitoun, Cairo, were the most interesting and most well documented. The apparitions were witnessed by Coptic bishops, including the Coptic Patriarch's representative, and witnessed by Christians, Muslims, Jews, and non-believers. The Coptic Church recognized the apparitions as true appearances of the Blessed Virgin Mary, as did the Greek Catholic Church and the Evangelical Church, which represented all the Protestant churches of Egypt.

Even the Egyptian government's director of general information submitted a report to his superior, stating that it was "an undeniable fact that the Blessed Virgin Mary has been appearing on Zeitoun Church in a clear and bright luminous body seen by all present in front of the church, whether Christians or Muslims."

When the vision appeared it was silent. There were no threats of punishment and no doomsday warnings, and no young girls were induced into trances and given secret messages. There were also no flashes of light or thunderous sounds. The apparition appeared on the domes of the church for up to two hours or more at a time, always at night, but not every night and not at regular times.

The Lady appeared in shining white light, so bright that her features could not be clearly seen. The apparition was preceded or accompanied by luminous disks that floated through the air and fell from the sky like leaves. The figure moved across the domes of the buildings bowing and greeting the enormous crowd that was estimated at times to be as many as fifty thousand people.

The representative of the church described the apparition as being "very quiet and full of glory." On at least one occasion the apparition appeared holding a child who many thought was the baby Jesus. Other types of phenomena that were reported when the "Lady" appeared were a "shower of diamonds," a glowing red cloud, and the smell of roses.

The next well-documented apparition took place in 1981 in Medjugorje, Bosnia and Herzegovina (then part of Yugoslavia). Once again the entity chose to pick children as contactees to induce trances and give secrets. Four teenagers, three girls and a boy all fifteen or sixteen years old, saw a white light and heard a "loud explosion" on a hillside one evening in June. In the light was a young woman holding a child. She called the children by name, but they ran away. The following evening they returned with two more friends, a girl of sixteen and a ten-year-old boy, and the woman appeared again, but this time on the opposite side of the hill. The apparition was surrounded by a bright white light as if she were "clothed with the sun."

After they told their story to the local police, their parents, and church officials, news of their "vision of the Madonna" quickly spread throughout the village and to the nearby towns.

The next evening the six youngsters were joined by thousands of people all desperately wanting to have a religious experience and witness a miracle. After three flashes of light and a loud roar, the female entity appeared again, but only the six youngsters could see her. The oldest girls described the being to a disappointed crowd who saw nothing as having dark hair, blue eyes, in a white dress with a crown of stars circling her head, standing on a silver cloud just above the ground.

The children told the crowd that she was so close they could have touched her. One of the girls said to the apparition, "If you are Satan, go away." The glowing, apparently female entity replied, *"I am the Virgin Mary, who has come to convert and reconcile all disbelievers."* Then a cross of rainbow-colored light appeared behind her. Once again this was only seen by the children. The apparition kept on repeating in a sad voice, *"Peace, peace, be reconciled."* The apparition then vanished with a flash of light and a low rumble of thunder.

Although the apparition was not witnessed by anyone else except the children, an unknown number of the thousands of people attending said they saw the flashes of light and heard a noise like the rumbling of thunder. The apparition appeared before the children every Sunday at about six p.m., but only if the rosary was recited. The apparition continued to appear over the next several months, and then was never seen again.

The oldest girl claimed the entity would appear to her at home, especially if she was praying. She was shown visions of Heaven, Hell, and Purgatory. The "Lady" also showed them visions of Heaven with angels in snow-white gowns flying through the air on gold wings praising God. She also was shown the souls of people who were in Heaven dressed in gray, pink, and yellow robes walking about, singing, and praying. In the fires of Hell she saw men and women emerging from a fiery pit of molten liquid unrecognizable as human beings.

The apparition also gave the oldest girl messages that called for peace in the world and the tolerance of all religious beliefs. The entity also said that God and Satan were engaged in a great battle for the souls of all people. The children continued to have visions of future events, but not one of the prophecies ever came true.

The former Roman Catholic Bishop of Mostar refused to accept the apparitions as genuine, but the Franciscan parish priest, Father Jozo Zovko, enthusiastically supported the young visionaries. Father Zovko was imprisoned by the Communist authorities for his activities in supporting the apparitions and convincing people they were a miracle sent by God.

Between 1981 and 1990, before the Bosnian conflict, ten million pilgrims from all over the world—including many Americans, Australians, and Europeans—came to Medjugorje on pilgrimages to pray and be healed. During that time a large numbers of pilgrims claimed to have seen Christ in the sky smiling down on them and the Virgin Mary floating on top of the clouds holding a child in her arms, which many thought was the baby Jesus.

One woman claimed her rosary had turned into gold, and every time she prayed it would glow like the sun. One person said that while taking pictures of the shrine area the Virgin Mary appeared in one of his pictures. This person claims the apparition was not visible to the eye and it was a miracle sent by God.

Since my interest in paranormal photography is great, I made it my business to take a look at this picture. It was sent to me recently by my friend Paulo, who'd had a copy of it for years. Thanks to the wonders of the Internet, the photograph was e-mailed to me as a JPEG in a matter of minutes.

Since the original negatives are no longer available, I cannot say for sure if it is a hoax or not. However, to me it looks like a double exposure, because the "Virgin Mary" looks like a popular statue that can be purchased at just about any store that sells religious items.

In 1993 four of the young people were still seeing visions. They claimed they saw the sun fall from the sky and move in circles. Mysterious glowing disks were seen shooting across the sky, and brilliant "rainbows" appeared without rain. Most fantastic of all, the word *MIR* (Peace) appeared over a mountain in letters of white light. This seems to have been witnessed by nearly everyone in Medjugorje, but what is even more amazing is that there are no pictures of this "miracle."

Many apparitions of the Virgin Mary were reported in Ukraine in the twentieth century. In 1987 the Virgin was said to have appeared in twenty different villages, and once again the targets of contact were teenage or pre-teen girls.

On April 26, 1987, a twelve-year-old Ukrainian girl named Marina saw a light above an abandoned, decaying chapel. A woman dressed in black, with a child in her arms, appeared in the light and said that Ukrainians had been chosen to lead the Russians back to God. The girl called her sister and mother, who immediately declared that it must be the Virgin Mary.

As news of the vision spread throughout the country, thousands of people came to see for themselves. Some claimed to have seen the apparition, but most could not and left disillusioned.

There was a rumor the apparition was imaged on May 13, 1987, by a camera crew from a local news station and shown on television. Unfortunately, the video was never broadcast in the United States. My attempts to find this video have been in vain. I even contacted a number of TV stations in Ukraine and received no reply.

During the visitation, the "Virgin Mary" would give messages sent by God. Although there were hundreds present during the vision, these messages were not heard by anyone except the young girl, Marina. The girl would appear to be in a trance and relay the messages to the crowd. The message from the "Lady" to Marina was the feeling of sorrow God had for the state of the world, and the end of days was soon approaching. After this, the apparition vanished and to my knowledge has not been seen since.

THE BAYSIDE APPARITIONS

In 1985 I heard through a number of sources, including a television broadcast, that Marian apparitions were being seen in the New York City borough of Queens. I was quite excited, since the location was within an hour's drive of where I was living at the time.

A group of people would meet in Flushing Meadows-Corona Park in Queens for a prayer vigil and experience manifestations they call miracles, but to me this means it could have a paranormal origin. This is very near the location of the 1964–65 New York World's Fair. The location was also made famous in the movie *Men in Black*.

Once a month the faithful would gather and claim to witness manifestations of Jesus, the Virgin Mary, and glowing angels in the sky (which sounded like UFOs to me). There were also claims of amazing photography—images that would appear on film, but were not seen with the eye. These psychic or paranormal photographic images varied from streaks of bright light to images of the Virgin Mary and Jesus. Several different saints, and even angels, would make an occasional appearance to get their picture taken.

Since the next meeting was still three weeks away, I still had time to do research and get some background information on the group and look into to some of their amazing claims.

The name of one witness to the "miracles" was given in the television broadcast. He lived in Queens, so I had no trouble finding him. I gave him a call, and to my surprise the gentleman had heard of me. It seems that he listened to a show I did about UFOs on a New York City radio station in 1984.

The witness to the "Miracle at Bayside" was thirty-two years old at the time, single, with deeply rooted Catholic beliefs. He believes what appeared in the sky that day while he attended the prayer vigil was an angel sent by God. His story appears below:

"This was the first time that I went to this group meeting. I had heard about it, but stayed away because the priest at my local church said he felt the devil was fooling people with tricks to get their confidence. Father John also told me the church did not sanction the group, and the so-called miracles were all fakes or tricks done by Satan. I had to see for myself, so the next meeting I attended. They are always outside in the park since hundreds of people show up. This was in March. The weather was cold, but people were so excited they didn't seem to care. It was Sunday at three p.m., and people were all singing and praying when the ministers of the group carried in the statue of the Virgin Mary. It was white marble or something like that, with a gold crown on her head and roses around the feet.

"One of the ministers said, 'Everyone pray.' He recited the Hail Mary about twenty times, and everyone gave their response. This went on for about fifteen minutes when some people pointed to the sky and yelled, '*Look!*'

"Everyone looked up and began to scream and fall to the ground on their knees. Out of the sky five bright lights appeared. They moved together in a circle for about thirty seconds, then just vanished—*poof!* They were gone. The lights were a gold color, and they were pretty high up and the formation they took was in a *V*. Everyone was crying and saying they were an army of angels showing us that God approved of what we were doing. I have to say it was amazing to see, and it made a believer out of me."

After asking him about a dozen follow-up questions, I thanked him and said goodbye. This was the time before the Internet, and getting information about this group and the alleged miracles was not an easy task.

HOW IT ALL BEGAN

The story of the "miracles" at Bayside began with a woman named Veronica Lueken, a mother of five children—one daughter and four sons. Veronica was married to a retired purchasing agent and led a perfectly normal life in New York City.

On June 5, 1968, Veronica broke down in tears when she heard the news that Robert F. Kennedy had been shot and was dying. It was during this time of great sorrow that she experienced the strong smell of roses. Veronica took this as a sign from God and prayed for the soul of the senator, who died the next day.

A week or so later, Saint Thérèse, who is always identified with roses, appeared to Veronica in her home.[18] The vision was supposedly also seen by her ten-year-old son, Raymond. Veronica's followers today claim the early visions of minor saints helped prepare her for the apparition that was to follow.

In 1970 Veronica claimed that the Virgin Mary (Our Lady of the Rosary) told her that she wanted rosary vigils held outdoors on the evenings of all the great Catholic feasts.[19]

These vigils were initially to be held on the grounds of the old Saint Bellarmine Church in the Bayside area of Queens. The apparition also told Veronica she wanted a shrine established at the location, and when her followers came to pray they could invoke her by calling, *"Our Lady of the Roses, Mary, Help of Mothers."*

The apparition promised that if the vigils were kept, even during adverse weather conditions, she would appear each time and display miracles to all those who were in doubt. The Lady also promised to give Veronica messages from God of worldwide importance. However, in order for this to

---

18. Saint Thérèse, also called Thérèse of Lisieux (1873–97), born Marie-Françoise-Thérèse Martin, was a French nun. She is also known as "The Little Rose Flower of Jesus." Saint Thérèse was canonized in 1925 by Pope Pius XI.

19. The number of Catholic feasts changes from year to year. On the average there are about twenty that are observed by Roman Catholics.

take place, prayers and the rosary must be said aloud continuously by all the people who attend.

Since that time in 1970, thousands of people have attended these vigils despite sometimes harsh weather conditions. Because the total number of people attending was increasing, in 1975 Veronica was instructed by the apparition to move the prayer vigil to its present location in Flushing Meadows.

During a number of the prayer sessions, followers claimed Veronica, acting as a "voice box," gave messages to the pilgrims from the Virgin Mary concerning future events. To my knowledge none of these prophecies ever came true. Although Veronica passed away in 1995, the vigil and prayer meetings continue at the time of the writing of this book.

MY INVESTIGATION

I discovered the next date of the vigil to be May 13 (1985), in the late afternoon. This was the feast of the Lady of Fátima, which seemed a good day to begin my investigation. Believing I was a prospective member, the group mailed me detailed information concerning their purpose and their fantastic claims of miracles.

Included in my introduction packet was a brochure with twenty-five images that were being passed off as "miracles." As I stated earlier, I have great interest in paranormal photography because, unlike verbal and written reports, photographs are something that can be analyzed.

In 1985 Photoshop and digital cameras for public purchase did not yet exist. All photographs taken during this time were done with print film and Polaroid instant cameras. I looked at each photograph, and most of the so-called miracle pictures in my opinion were double exposures, obvious fakes.

One of the images showed a statue of the Virgin Mary with the face of Saint Francis of Assisi in the background. It was my opinion that the face of the saint was photographed from a painting and superimposed over a negative of the statue to make it look like a manifestation was taking place in the background.

There was, however, a number of images taken by the people who attended the vigil that showed streaks of light that appear to be flashing and doing maneuvers. The leaders of the "Bayside Miracles" claim that these images are angels flying around the crowd keeping out the "devil" and checking who is faithful and who is not. There was no information on how the pictures were taken or what type of camera was used. I centered my investigation on these alleged paranormal images that, according to the brochure, were taken independently by members of the crowd.

As the afternoon of May 13 approached, I got my gear together and drove down to Queens to witness the alleged miracles for myself. It was a cloudy, damp day with plenty of rain in the forecast, but the organizers clearly state in their brochure that the vigils are never canceled.

I arrived early, and to my surprise hundreds of people were already present, waiting for the event to begin. I took my place among the crowd and began to mingle. The weather was cold, and at times the rain would come pouring down. This did not stop the people who attended; they seemed almost driven into ecstasy by the rain. It reminded me of one of many familiar Catholic beliefs that I heard as a youth in Sunday school: *When you suffer for God, you get his attention.*

I asked a middle-aged woman if they were going to cancel because of the weather. She replied, "Of course not. We must come every Catholic feast and pray; otherwise no more miracles will take place." This comment made it sound as though this was the price people pay to get an evening of supernatural entertainment. The woman then said, "At times the Lady will create the severe weather just to test our faith."

I did not agree with her. Why would a benevolent ascended being want to see lower life forms suffer?

The suffering bit never really made much sense to me, unless of course the apparition is not who she claims to be. The purpose of my visit was to conduct research and not to get into discussions or debates, so I kept my opinions to myself.

I personally do not believe that the creator of the universe or any ascended being would want to watch us poor humans suffer for their personal amusement or to test our resolve. One would think they would be above that sort of mentality. This made be consider that some type of entity other than God or angels was responsible for the manifestations.

Since there were multiple sightings of UFOs during the vigils, I had to consider that some type of alien beings might be responsible for the so-called miracles. The question that many might ask is: why would an alien intelligence want to gather hundreds of people at one location?

UFO investigators who research the abduction phenomenon would probably say it was a good way to get large
groups of people together in a small area, and scan them to
discover compatible human beings who fill their needs. The
selected ones could be abducted at a future date far from the
crowds.

The rain continued to fall from the sky with increasing
intensity. Despite my rain gear and an umbrella I was getting very wet. As I waited for the beginning of the activities, five large buses jam-packed with people pulled into the
parking area. In a short time the field was packed shoulder
to shoulder with muddy, wet people holding rosary beads. I
would say that at least half the people present had cameras.

THE ENTRANCE

I noticed the majority of cameras were of the instant type.
This simply means you push a button, and the film comes
out the front and develops within several minutes. As I
looked around, it seemed that everyone with an "instant"
camera had the same model—the Polaroid SX-70! The SX-
70 was a camera that instantly developed pictures and was
produced from 1972 until 1981.[20] I would find out very soon
this was more than just a coincidence.

The festivities began with a number of men and women
unloading a statue of the Virgin Mary from a truck. In slow
precession, they carried the effigy in front of the crowd and

20. Robert Hirsch, *Exploring Color Photography*, 5th edition (Focal Press:
    2011), 27.

placed it on a wooden stage draped with colorful material that had images of red roses.

As the statue was centered and secured on the stage, everyone in the crowd began saying the Hail Mary, a prayer I knew very well from my younger days, as I was raised in a Roman Catholic family.

Many of the people began putting their hands up in the air, seemingly hoping to touch God or one of the many angels they believed were floating around. The crowd continued to recite the prayer to the Virgin Mary. With the beginning of each new verse, they chanted louder and louder:

Hail Mary, full of grace
The Lord is with thee
Blessed are you among women
Blessed is the fruit of thy womb, Jesus
Holy Mary, Mother of God
Pray for us sinners
Now and at the hour of our death
Amen

The sky was still overcast and the rain continued to come down steadily. I walked close to the effigy, which was adorned with roses, and I was quite surprised to see it was not made of marble, as is the case with most statuettes of this nature, but inexpensive plastic.

People attempted to light candles, but the rain snuffed them out. To replace the effect made by lighting candles, many people brought flashlights and turned them on.

At least half the people who attended were dressed in jumpsuits with a white beret on their head. I found out later those who were in this uniform were the full-time members of the group, who dedicated their life and property to the leaders of the group.

Everyone with cameras started photographing the statue of Mary with their instant cameras. I looked at several of the results and saw streaks of light across the photographs. In many cases the image was blurry; this was the beginning of the answer as to what produced the mysterious images.

I asked several of the photographers if they ever got any of the streaks of light or anything else unusual with a different type of camera. One woman said to me, "You have to use this type of camera or no miracles will appear, and for your information, sir, *they are not streaks of light but angels!*" It wasn't my intention to get into an argument with this person, so I continued to walk among the crowd and looked at some of the pictures others had taken.

In some of the photographs there was nothing unusual, just people with flashlights. In some other photographs there were people with streaks of light around them. Finally, in others there were blurry images of people, the landscape, and multicolored streaks of light extending from the flashlights.

Although in my opinion the images showed nothing more than light streaks from the flashlights as a result of camera movement, every photographer claimed they had photographed angels.

Then without warning there was a sound like rolling thunder. I have to admit it took me by surprise and made me jump, since the rumbling didn't sound like thunder but more like an earthquake. Almost immediately after the thunder it stopped raining, and a break in the clouds appeared. Although at this time the sun should have been well to the west, a ray of light shined down from the clouds and illuminated the statue. It was at this time that a woman, one of the leaders on stage, claimed she heard the Virgin Mary's voice. The crowd became silent. It's a good thing she was using a loudspeaker and I had my trusty tape recorder. This is what she said during her contact session:

THE MESSAGE

"The Lady of the Rosary is talking to me. She wants to give you all a message from Jesus our Lord. Today He made it rain in order to find those whose faith is untouched by the weather. The end of the world as you know it is coming soon, and all must reach out to Heaven for salvation and forgiveness. The devil comes in many guises, and this is his day on Earth. You must not only show love for your family but also spread this feeling throughout the world. You must also love God the most, for He is the only chance for you to survive the great tribulation that is about to unfold. Many of you will have visions, and through me I will give you strength and teach you the rosary and prayers to say to God. The ray of light you see today did not come from the sun, but from Heaven. It is the light of one thousand angels creating a shield to protect you all from the evil that lies outside this special circle. Be loyal to this ministry and always attend the prayer vigils on the holiest of days. The way to Heaven is through Jesus, for He is the true son of God and will soon take His place as king of the earth."

After the message, the woman collapsed on the stage. Luckily, two men standing close caught her before she fell off. To me it looked like it was all staged. Had she actually fallen off the stage it would have made this alleged contact experience more believable. The two men seemed ready to act as if following a script.

Five minutes after the message, the sky once again darkened and again we were all standing in pouring rain. Despite pools of water and mud on the ground, people dropped to their knees and prayed. I was soaked right down to my undergarments and could not wait to get home to a dry place, so I left.

The next day I came down with strep throat and was sick for two full weeks. My doctor kept on switching antibiotics, because whatever I had was resistant to all the drugs prescribed. The pain was so bad that I could not eat solid food for a week and drank from a straw. Finally, with massive doses of antibiotics and lots of rest, the illness faded away and I was back to my old self.

Later, a member of the Queens Marian group would tell me the infection was punishment from God for trying to expose legitimate Marian sightings as a hoax. Sorry, folks, this time it wasn't the wrath of God, just being out in the wet, damp cold for several hours without the proper clothing.

A POSSIBLE SOLUTION

The next step was to concentrate on the mysterious streaks of light that appeared on the photographs taken with the Polaroid SX-70. It was time to do extensive research on the camera and try to duplicate the so-called angels.

The SX-70 had several problems: the first was if you pressed on the film while it was developing, the image could become distorted. Rings can appear across the photograph, and if bent in the early stages of developing, bright streaks will appear on the final print. However, the developing-flaw bright streaks were much different from the ones photographed at the vigil. It was my opinion that these "angel" light streaks were something external rather than internal.

I got ahold of an SX-70 camera and began to experiment. I discovered something quite interesting that could explain the "angel light" streaks on the film taken by the vigil attendees.

The SX-70 automatically adjusts to the light available. This means if it is very bright out, the shutter opens and closes quickly. If it is dark, the shutter will stay open for at least a second to compensate for the low light. This was probably why so many of the pictures taken by people at the vigil that day were blurred. The shutter was still open when they began to move the camera. The streaks of light therefore could have been produced by people walking and waving their flashlights.

I returned to the site of the vigil the following month with an assistant. I picked a day when I was sure no one would be there. Using only a small pen light, my assistant and I were able to duplicate the streaks of light with no statue of the Virgin Mary or crowd present. The streaks were not almost like what people got; they were exactly identical.

My conclusions were that there was no psychic or paranormal photography taking place at these vigils. The images published in their journals of Jesus and the saints appearing behind the effigy were obvious double exposures. The streaks of light obtained by the attendees were nothing more than flashlights and candles moving quickly past an open camera shutter.

I could not explain the strange thunderous sound, the ray of light, or why the rain stopped during the channeled message and started again after it was finished. I could not find an explanation for the apparent UFO sightings that had been reported during the vigils, but at that time they were being spotted all over the New York area. UFOs were being seen in areas where there were no prayer vigils, no churches, and no statues of the Virgin Mary.

In December of that year I published a story in a New York Sunday magazine about the "Miracles in Queens," revealing my findings from my investigation. In the weeks to follow I received thirty-three letters from irate dedicated followers of the Marian group accusing me of being in league with the devil.

This was a surprise to me, since the Lady of the Rosary (the Virgin Mary) represents peace and love. If they were true followers of the Lady and followed what she stood for, then why would they threaten me? Even after more than twenty-five years I am still quite shocked by how the group reacted to my story. Over the years I have exposed or written negatively about many occult groups in New York and New England. However, the response I got from these so-called people of God was much more severe than the Satanist groups in the same region.

A final note: In 1992 the Catholic Church in New York officially announced, much to the dismay of the followers, that they do not endorse the visions or miracles of Bayside and Corona Park.

CONCLUSIONS

Apparitions of religious figures are quite common. But only a very small percentage of them have any real documentation. The entity seems to pick young children, especially girls, to contact. Most adults see or hear nothing, and most of the information given by the entity is relayed to the audience from the channel.

My research has shown that the greatest number of people who claim alien abduction and psychic contact from ultraterrestrials or extraterrestrials are young women and teenage girls. Perhaps the brains of human females are wired differently from those of men to accept this type of communication. Is it also just a coincidence that most people who claim they can channel angels or other non-earthly beings are women?

Finally, if God, Jesus, Mary, and the saints are all behind the apparitions, don't you think that a highly ascended being could find a more efficient and convincing way to do so? Also, why are there no apparitions reported of Moses, Muhammad, Vishnu, or Buddha?

Many of the cases presented earlier in this chapter are similar in the sense that a bright light is seen and a sound like thunder is heard before the apparition appears and vanishes. Also, in many of the cases, UFO-like objects were seen in the sky. UFO investigators would explain the apparitions and other phenomena as some type of contact with an alien race.

It is my belief the apparitions of religious figures are caused by entities such as *djinn*. In the Western world we are only familiar with human beings, angels, and fallen angels, which have often been referred to as demons. However, in the Muslim belief there is a third race that is much older than the human race. The Qur'an makes it very clear that the djinn existed before humanity, but just how long before no one seems to know for sure.

The word *djinn*, or *jinn* (or *djinni* for individual djinn), can be traced to the Arabic word *janna*, or *jannu*, which simply means "hidden." This implies the djinn are invisible to humans unless they want to be seen. According to Islamic belief, the race of djinn live in desolate locations. These places are said to be haunted or cursed, so the people kept away from these locations fear that they might invite the wrath of a djinni for invading its privacy.

In modern terms, the invisibility of the djinn and living in a distant, hidden, and desolate place could mean they exist in a parallel dimension that is close to our own reality. They are out of reach and cannot be seen in the normal sense. It makes one wonder if shadow-like beings that are reported around the world are djinn spying on us by pressing against the membrane that divides their world from ours. In the Western world we have little knowledge of this ancient race, but they have been mentioned in the media and some literature as the *genie*.

The people of the Middle East in both ancient and modern times consider the djinn very dangerous and uncontrollable. The Qur'an states that, like human beings, djinn have free will and can choose between good and evil. This simply means not all djinn are evil; some are good and many are indifferent and don't want to be bothered by humans. The Qur'an has an entire *surah* (division) dedicated to the djinn called *Al-Jinn*.

Djinn do not have a physical form, but they can take a number of different shapes. To go unnoticed, djinn like to take the shape of a human or an animal. The mountain people of Oman believe you can tell a djinni from a human by looking into their eyes. Although they can mimic the human body, they have difficulty with the eyes. The eyes of a djinni would be yellow with elongated pupils. Perhaps in many cases a djinni might take a form that is pleasing to the person they contact in order to get their confidence. The true purpose of these communications is unknown. Perhaps it is a young djinni or similar entity playing their favorite game—fool the human!

CHAPTER 7

HAUNTED PLACES

There are many places in North America where paranormal phenomena have been reported. The majority of these locations are said to be haunted by the ghosts of Native Americans or soldiers who died violently in battle. Some think these haunted places are the homes of nature spirits, such as the Algonquin Trickster, who protect their territory with an unbridled passion.

Yet, there are those who think that many of these locations are the domain of malevolent spirits like demons or djinn, who lies in waiting like a spider in its web for some susceptible human to fall into its trap. Such a creature might feed on fear and take on a number of terrifying forms. It may be able to read the mind of its victim and assume a shape that would induce the most terror. In other words, an entity like the one described above knows what scares you. This could be the reason why monsters of a variety of descriptions are reported in these haunted or cursed lands.

Many of these places have already been presented by other authors over and over again. They include Gettysburg, Camelback Mountain, Mount Shasta, the Bell Witch Cave, and the Bermuda and Bridgewater Triangles—just to name a few out of hundreds. Although I have personally visited some of the most haunted locations in America, many of the well-known ones will not be covered in this chapter. It is my intention to present those haunted places that are not very well known, even to the most seasoned paranormal researchers.

A HISTORY OF TRAUMA

Although many places in New England are haunted, most of the towns in this region keep the strange goings-on in their backyard quiet. A great deal of New England and New York saw considerable action during the Revolutionary War. Many of the locations in which battles with the British were fought must have left a residue of psychic energy behind. However, it was more than the fighting that killed the colonial soldiers; they were also constantly struggling to stay alive in very adverse conditions.

The history books are filled with heroic stories of brave colonials defending their land against the tyranny of King George III of Great Britain. During the Revolutionary War, a considerable number of colonists remained loyal to the British crown. After the war these people were labeled as traitors; however, loyalists, as they were called, considered the rebels traitors to Britain.

Today we remember George Washington as a great hero who won the war against Britain, freed the colonies from tyrannical rule, and became the father of our country. I wonder how Washington would be remembered today if the colonies had lost the war. Perhaps in another reality Great Britain did win the war, and the history books in this parallel world remember George Washington as well as all the founding fathers of United States as rebels and traitors. The history of war is, of course, written by the victorious.

During the Revolutionary War, American troops had to suffer great hardships. The short supply of food, clothes, and medicine made the war a horrible experience for almost all the soldiers. This resulted in countless numbers of soldiers dying from disease, exposure, and starvation. For the average foot soldier during the American Revolution, the suffering was great. This could be the reason why ghostly images of colonial soldiers are reported in New England's most haunted places.

MEN LONG AGO, GHOSTS TODAY

Putnam Memorial State Park is named after Major General Israel Putnam, who chose the site as an encampment for his troops during the winter of 1778–79. The park is located in the town of Redding, Connecticut, and is one of many locations in that area where paranormal phenomena are frequently reported.

One of the amazing things about the park is that it is loaded with many boulders pushed down from Hudson Bay during the last ice age. The boulders are piled on top of each other, forming rock shelters and small caves. It is here, in one of these rock shelters, that the most popular ghost story of the park began.

Before we get into the paranormal happenings, let's cover more about the troops who were stationed there during what was one of the coldest winters ever recorded. This will give the reader a greater understanding why the park is so psychically charged today.

General Putnam's troops had very little shelter. They would gather together around campfires during the long, cold nights and huddle together to keep warm. The stone circles that marked the containment rings of the fires can still be seen today. The living conditions were very poor: no shelter from the elements; the food supply was short; and many soldiers only had the clothes that they brought with them from home. General Putnam himself did not stay in the camp and really didn't seem to care what his troops were going through.

One of the only surviving documents comes from the journals of Private Joseph Plumb Martin. It shows the desperate lack of food and poor weather conditions endured by the troops throughout January 1779:

"We settled in our winter quarters at the commencement of the New Year and went on in our old Continental Line of starving and freezing. We now and then got a little bad bread and salt beef. I believe chiefly horse-beef, for it was generally thought to be such at the time. The month of January was very stormy, a good deal of snow fell, and in such weather it was mere chance if we got anything at all to eat."[21]

Just like most generals at that time, Putnam did not stay with his troops and endure the hardships with them. The general stayed at a nearby farmhouse and had shelter, a warm bed, and good food while his men suffered. Historians at Putnam Park think his headquarters were on what is now known as Limekiln Road, owned by a gentleman by the name of Samuel Gold. Other historians think Putnam stayed in a house that is no longer standing, on Umpawaug Hill Road.[22]

It's not surprising that many paintings of him from that time show a man who was more than slightly overweight. Many of the generals in the Revolutionary War came from prominent rich families, and some had close friends in the Continental Congress. They had a great deal to gain at the end of the war. There is no coincidence that these leaders and generals ended up with large plots of land after the war. When the war ended, many of the soldiers went home to find their property and homes destroyed or confiscated by the newly formed government of the United States.

During the encampment at what is now Putnam Park, an unknown number of soldiers died of exposure and sickness. At least seven of them were buried just off the park trail in an

---

21. From a copy of a letter displayed at Putnam Memorial Park, Redding, Connecticut. State of Connecticut historical document archive PP: Joseph Plumb-01.

22. John Fiske, "Putnam, Israel." *Appleton's Encyclopedia of American Biography* (1899).

area that today is marked as a possible cemetery. It is thought that many more died and their graves were scattered across the park's 183 acres. Since the British were already in nearby Danbury, Putnam knew he would have to move his troops soon. He ordered no grave markers, since he did not want the British to know just how many men he lost.

In addition to the deaths from exposure during the harsh winter encampment, according to General Putnam's diary there were also soldiers who deserted. Although the actual number of men who did desert and got away is unknown, those who were caught were hanged in a nearby place that is known today as Gallows Hill.

We now have all the background information required to understand why the park is a very hot place for ghost sightings and other strange otherworldly occurrences.

MY VISITS

I have been to Putnam Park many times and have walked the trails both during the day and at night. The place has a depressing feeling, as if a great deal of hardship and pain took place there, which of course it did.

During archeological digs over the years, a considerable number of artifacts have been found in the park. They include buttons from uniforms, pans, cups, parts of rifles, cannons, several decayed cabins, and finally a number of tools. Most of the smaller artifacts that have been found are now displayed in a beautiful new museum on the grounds.

My first visit to Putnam Memorial Park was in the spring of 1981. When I asked the museum curator about ghost sightings, he laughed and shied away from the question. During that time period, most people, especially in Connecticut, did not want to believe in otherworldly things like spirits of the dead, UFOs, or anything having to do with the paranormal. It is no wonder why the state is called "the land of steady habits."

In 2009 I returned to the park. I asked once again about ghosts, but this time the museum curator was very willing to discuss staff and visitors' experiences with paranormal events in the park. As a matter of fact, every October since 2005 they have been sponsoring evening ghost walks through the park. On these walks, a local historian carrying an old-fashioned lantern tells his paying guests stories of the many spooky legends and ghost sightings that have taken place since colonial days.

After my visit to the museum, I walked the grounds. There was a heavy feeling in the air, and one could sense the trauma experienced by the colonial soldiers over two hundred years before. I had walked the lonely trails many times over the years, and although I witnessed no paranormal events that crisp day in October, I did find the place worthy to visit again sometime in the near future, armed with my research equipment.

GHOSTS OF PUTNAM PARK

In order to have ghost tours, you must have ghosts. For years the administrators of the park tried to play down the many ghost encounters that people had on the trails during the day and night. However, since "ghost hunting" has become a popular pastime and made it big on reality television, the people in charge at Putnam Memorial Park must have figured it was a good way to raise money. They were right!

When I first found out they were offering ghost tours it surprised me, since the town had always been very conservative about the paranormal. I have never been on one of their tours, but plan to do so next Halloween. Let me present several of the ghost sightings that made the park a popular place to look for the world of the phantasm.

REVOLUTIONARY PHANTOMS

Whether they know the history of Putnam Park or not, every person I know always reports an eerie feeling while walking the trails. Over the years I have collected a great number of encounters with ghostly apparitions from those who have visited and walked on those trails of sorrow.

During the summer of 1993 a senior couple decided to go for an early Saturday morning walk at Putnam Park. As they walked the trails, they noticed a man in the distance coming toward them. As he got closer, they realized the man was dressed "like a Revolutionary War soldier." They stopped as the man got close and asked him, "Hi, is there a show going on today?" The man gave the couple a "funny" look and increased his pace as he walked past them.

Thinking they may have insulted the man in some way, they turned around to say goodbye, but he was gone. The couple insisted that he disappeared as soon as he passed them. Was this a ghost of a soldier who died during the encampment, or one of those rare times when the past and present cross together, allowing both realities to coexist?

THE RESTLESS DEAD

While walking on the trails in the park, you will pass by what historians believe was a graveyard to bury those men who died from exposure during the 1778–79 winter encampment. On more than one occasion visitors have reported seeing phantoms standing by the alleged gravesites; some are even crying. In most cases I investigated, the "phantoms" were dressed in clothes dating back to the eighteenth century. In all of the reports, witnesses said the "ghosts" just vanished when approached. However, in one particular report that came to my attention in 1988, the single witness, a man in his mid-fifties, reported:

"I was walking on the trail and came to the location where they say an unknown number of colonial soldiers are buried. I saw one individual standing on the grass and looking down to the ground. He looked like he was dressed in unusual clothes that were dirty and ragged. I didn't say anything and just walked by him and didn't look back. Later I thought the entire experience was quite unusual. I began to wonder if I actually saw a ghost. I didn't think he was a ghost at the time because the man looked solid and it was in the late afternoon in August. Every ghost story I ever heard always takes place at night, but now I wonder."

THE GALLOWS HILL SPOOK LIGHT

Besides the lack of shelter and provisions, General Putnam and his officers were most annoyed during the encampment by the desertions that had thinned the ranks and the loyalist spies who occasionally infiltrated his camps in the guise of farmers bringing food to the troops. While feeding Putnam's hungry troops, the "farmers" would ask all kinds of questions about troop strength, locations, and supplies. They would later convey this information to the British and were paid handsomely for their services. To put a stop to this, it had been determined that the next offender(s) would suffer death as an example to others.

On February 4, 1779, a Connecticut man named Edmond Jones was tried and found guilty of being a spy. He was sentenced to death. Two days later, on February 6, 1779, John Smith of the 1st Connecticut Regiment was found guilty of desertion, and also sentenced to death.

General Putnam decided that executing both men at once would be more efficient and set an example to future spies and deserters. He gave an order to "make a double job of it." The hill on the southwest side of the camp was chosen as the place of the executions. Both men ended up being hanged, since Putnam did not want to waste precious weaponry by using a firing squad. The place where the hangings took place became known to the soldiers as "Gallows Hill."

After the hangings, every soldier under Putnam's command was ordered to march by and look at the mangled remains.[23] Today in Redding this area is a long stretch of winding country road called Gallows Hill Road. Here, ever since the nineteenth century, there have been reports of globes of light—a phenomenon often associated with ghosts called "spook light."

People who drive on the street or live there have reported orbs of light that float alongside of the road, above the trees and into the woods. There have also been reports of voices of men screaming in the night or crying in pain. The voices seem to be disembodied and are heard in the wintertime and never in the summer. According to local folklore, the lights are ghosts of the men hanged on Gallows Hill, searching for a way to prove their innocence so they can be free and enter Heaven.

THE GHOST OF "PHILLIPS' CAVE"

Off one of the main trails is an area of large boulders that form a number of small rock shelters. Local legend says one of these small caves was used by a man whose last name was Phillips, first name unknown.

Phillips was a soldier under the command of General Putnam and was stationed at Redding, in what is now Putnam Park, during the harsh winter of 1778–79. According to local history and park historians, Phillips returned to the site of his former encampment after the war to live in this cave. He led the life of a hermit, stealing vegetables or an

---

23. Charles Todd, *The History of Redding* (Redding Historical Society, 1906).

occasional chicken from local farmers. After several years the farmers got fed up with his thievery, and Phillips was evicted by the community.

Another version said he was "permanently removed." The word *permanently* used before *removed* bothered me. After questioning local historians and searching through a great number of documents, I came to the conclusion Phillips may have been murdered by the local constable and farmers.

In one version of the story, they waited for him to return to the cave from one of his many raids at the expense of the local farmers. The group of men captured Phillips and hanged him in the park. They buried his body in a secret location.

In another version of the story, the farmers and constable arrived at the cave when Phillips was in it, sleeping. They hid outside the cave among some of the many stones near the cave's entrance. As Phillips woke up and walked out of the cave they ambushed him, shot him dead, and buried his body somewhere in the park's 187 acres. Another account of the Phillips story was written by Connecticut historian Odell Shepard in 1939:

> *What is the inward meaning and explanation . . . of that pathetic legend they tell in Redding, at the Putnam Memorial Camp, about "Phillips' Cave"? The bare facts are, apparently, that sometime after the winter of 1778–79 when several hundred Revolutionary soldiers encamped there under the leadership of Israel Putnam—one can still see the scattered stones of their fireplaces stretching in long straight lines down the*

hill—one of these soldiers, Phillips by name, wandered back to the place and lived alone there for a time in a cave among the tumbled rocks. He lived at first, as his old comrades had done, upon the game he could kill, then upon alms, and at last upon what pigs and poultry he could steal. Tiring of his depredations, farmers of the region lay in wait for him one evening and shot him dead as he came out of his cave. [24]

Today, visitors who walk by "Phillips' Cave" claim to have seen him sitting in the dark. There are also reports of hikers on the trails seeing a man walking along the stones and entering the cave. Some have reported a vagabond walking the trails during the day and night only to vanish in a flash of light.

The ghosts of Putnam Park are well known in the folklore of Connecticut. If by chance you visit, please be sure to stop in the museum and talk to the curator about the strange happenings that have been reported on the grounds. As I mentioned, I have found that park employees are more willing to discuss the paranormal aspects of the park today than they were twenty-five years ago.

DEVIL'S HOPYARD

No fewer than thirty-four places in Connecticut are associated with the devil by legend or name. The most popular is Devil's Hopyard in East Haddam, an 860-acre state park with waterfalls, caves, and a very spooky forest. According

---

24. Odell Shepard, *Connecticut Past and Present* (Knopf, 1939).

to local folklore that dates back to the late seventeenth century, the Hopyard is or was the place in which the devil and his demons enter our world. According to colonial tales, the devil loved to sit by the many waterfalls and stare at the water cascading over the rocks and splashing in the pond below. Some say that when he needed a break from Hell he would enter our world through a dark doorway that opened in the Hopyard near the falls. Here the devil would stay for hours watching the water.

On a warm spring day the sight was so beautiful that it reminded the demon of his glorious days in Heaven as an angel. After a torrential rainstorm the devil came into our world to visit his favorite place. The water level was unusually high, and he didn't want to get his feet wet so he turned his legs into blazing fire and evaporated the water as he walked to his favorite spot near the falls. The heat was so great that it burned holes in the bedrock that are still there today. The legend does not say when the holes in the ground first appeared. According to my research, they have been there since the park was first explored by Europeans sometime in the mid-seventeenth century.

The potholes are unique in appearance and much different from any formations that I have seen in the Western Hemisphere or any other part of the world. The potholes are perfectly cylindrical; they range from inches to several feet in diameter. On the average each pothole is about twelve inches deep. According to a geologist at the University of Connecticut, the potholes were formed by stones that were moved downstream by water currents and trapped in an eddy where the stone was spun around and around, wearing a depression in the rock. When the rock wore itself down, another would catch in the same hole and enlarge it.

Although this explanation is only theoretical, it is accepted by local residents and most geologists. However, to the early settlers of Connecticut the potholes were a great mystery. In one of many stories concerning their formation, they believed the devil passed by the falls and accidentally got his tail wet. This made the demon so mad that he burned holes in the bedrock with his hooves as he walked away. The state of Connecticut uses the mystery to entice people to visit the park.

"Could the round holes in the falls really be the work of the devil? Or, just nature and water making their mark for future generations? Visit Devil's Hopyard and find your own answer to this age-old mystery."[25]

THE DEVIL'S ALE

My search for historical records for the origin of the name *Devil's Hopyard* revealed a wide variety of different stories; none of them are verifiable, and all are likely to be more fiction than fact. One of the most popular of these stories is about a man named Dibble, who in 1689 had a garden for growing hops used in the brewing of ale. In 1699 the area was known as Dibble's Hopyard, and sometime in 1726 it became the Devil's Hopyard.

---

25. "Devil's Hopyard State Park," State of Connecticut Department of Energy & Environmental Protection website, http://www.ct.gov/dep/cwp/view.asp?a=2716&q=325188.

There are documented records of several farmers who owned land in and around the park, but there is no mention of a landowner named Dibble. However, Dibble might not have owned the land; he could have rented it. If this was the case, Dibble's name would not show up in a landowners search.

It is clear now how the place got its name. It was once a place where hops were grown for ale, and it was believed to be the entrance point of Satan in this world. This led to strange stories that Dibble made a deal with the devil, and as payment the demon would collect his fee once a month in ale.

STRANGE HAPPENINGS IN THE HOPYARD

Over the past two centuries people who hike the trails have reported seeing shadow-like beings that appear on the trail and stare at them, scaring them away. Ghostlike phantoms have allegedly been seen moving around the woodland. Sightings of a Bigfoot-like creature have also been reported since the eighteenth century. This creature was, and is still today, known as the "Wild Man of the Hopyard."

Native American legends say that Devil's Hopyard is the home of a very powerful spirit who would punish anyone who trespassed on his land without an offering. In the early twentieth century local residents stayed out of the woods, since they believed that anyone who entered and stayed would eventually go mad.

In 1910 hikers and hunters reported a "large black ghost dog" that appeared on the trails and chased people out. Bullets would knock the animal down when it was fired upon, but then several seconds later it would get up unharmed and continue pursuing the hunters. The ghost dog would chase them to a point at the end of the trail and then vanish.

In more recent times, people who travel the isolated areas of the woods have allegedly photographed multicolored orbs and mists that often take on human form. Everyone I talked with reported that while walking the trails they had strong feelings of foreboding and being watched. Others have heard demonic-sounding voices and inexplicable laughing coming from the woods. Also, I am aware of at least two photographic images that show a small gnome-like creature running through the woods.

During my visit, as I walked through the woods and approached Chapman Falls, I felt this was not an evil place, but a mystical and magical one. At times I almost expected to see an elf, gnome, or some other mythical being sitting or sunbathing on the rocks. What intrigued me most is the reference of a black doorway by which the devil and his demons enter our world. This sounds like a dimensional portal.

As of 2012 there have been reports of hikers hearing unusual humanlike and animal sounds coming from the forest. A number of ghost-hunting enthusiasts in Connecticut claim to have received electronic voice phenomena (EVP). The EVP consisted of a number of messages, and most were threatening in nature. Although I have not heard the recordings, it stimulated my interest to visit the Hopyard in the near future with a wide range of equipment. I hope I will be able to produce documented evidence to settle the debate about whether or not Devil's Hopyard is a paranormal hotbed.

CHAPTER 8

GHOSTS OF THE ALAMO

In the mid-1970s I lived in San Antonio. As a resident of that beautiful south-central Texas city, I went many times to its most famous landmark—the Alamo.

Walking through the old mission and fort for the first time, I felt quite uneasy. The atmosphere seemed charged, for lack of a better word. You could feel the psychic impressions of the great battle that took place there in 1836. This feeling was much more than the power of suggestion; it has been reported by everyone I know who has visited the Texas shrine. This feeling was as if a thin veil or web encompassed the halls, something you would rather avoid than walk through. I heard the comments of many who were touring that hot June day, saying it felt "cold and sad," and some said they just had a bad feeling and wanted to leave.

HISTORY OF THE ALAMO

Originally the Alamo was named *Mission San Antonio de Valero* and served as home to missionaries and their Indian converts for nearly seventy years. The main structure was constructed in 1724 and was used as a church for the growing community of San Antonio.

In the early 1800s the Spanish military stationed a cavalry unit at the former mission. The soldiers referred to the mission as the Alamo in honor of Álamo de Parras, in Coahuila. The post's commander established the first recorded hospital in Texas in the Long Barrack.

San Antonio and the Alamo played a critical role in the Texas Revolution. In December 1835, Benjamin Milam led Texan and Tejano volunteers against Mexican troops quartered in the city.[26] After five days of house-to-house fighting, they forced General Martín Perfecto de Cos and his soldiers to surrender. The victorious volunteers then occupied the Alamo and fortified its walls. Volunteers came from throughout southern Texas and from as far away as Tennessee to help hold it from the counterattack of the approaching Mexican army. General Sam Houston ordered Colonel William B. Travis to hold the fort.

On February 23, 1836, the arrival of General Antonio López de Santa Anna's six-thousand-man army caught them by surprise, since they believed the attacking force would be much smaller.

---

26. *Tejano* is a Texan of Mexican descent. The term is still used today in southern Texas.

William B. Travis, the commander of the Alamo, sent forth couriers asking for help to communities in Texas. On the eighth day of the siege, a band of thirty-two volunteers from the settlement of Gonzales arrived, bringing the number of defenders to nearly two hundred.

With the possibility of additional help fading, Travis drew a line on the ground and asked any man willing to stay and fight to step over; all except one did so. As the defenders saw it, the Alamo was the key to the defense of Texas, and they were ready to give their lives rather than surrender their position to General Santa Anna. Among the Alamo's garrison were Jim Bowie and David Crockett. Greatly outnumbered, the defenders were able to hold out for thirteen days.

The final assault came before daybreak on the morning of March 6, 1836, as columns of Mexican soldiers emerged from the predawn darkness and headed for the Alamo's walls. Cannon and small arms fire from inside the Alamo beat back several attacks. The Mexicans retreated, reformed their ranks, and attacked again. This time they were able to reach the walls, scale them, and rush into the compound. Once inside, they turned a captured cannon on the Long Barracks and church and blasted open the barricaded doors.

The desperate struggle continued until the defenders were overwhelmed. By sunrise the battle had ended and Santa Anna, riding a jet-black horse, entered the Alamo to look over the results of his victory.

WHAT HAPPENED TO THE BODIES?

The bodies of the Mexican soldiers were buried at the old Campo Santo cemetery near what is known today as Milam Park. Santa Anna ordered the bodies of the Alamo defenders to be burned. The exact location of the funeral fires seems to have been lost with the passage of time. One source, a document displayed at the Alamo, indicates that a large fire was lit in the middle of the compound and the bodies were piled on it and burned to bone and ash. That would place it somewhere in what is today the Alamo Plaza. The remains were buried somewhere within the land that surrounds the Alamo.[27]

A LONG PARANORMAL HISTORY

Over the years many skeptics and believers alike have experienced startling unexplained paranormal phenomena at the Alamo. Some of these events can be explained as the product of overactive imaginations, but most cannot. There are many other famous haunted battlefields where paranormal phenomena are reported, but the Alamo is arguably the best-known and most active of these places in the United States.

Ghostly stories at the Alamo can be traced back to 1836. Three weeks after the siege of the Alamo, Santa Anna ordered one of his generals to destroy the Alamo to ensure

27. Antonio Francisco Ruiz, "Fall of the Alamo, and Massacre of Travis and His Brave Associates," in *The Texas Almanac, 1857–1873* (Texan Press, 1967), 357.

that it could not be used again as a fort. Just like military commanders today, the general delegated what he considered a task below his rank to a subordinate by the name of Colonel Sanchez.

Colonel Sanchez and forty soldiers pulled down the remaining walls and barriers until all that remained of the old mission was the chapel. Being a religious man, he had a bad feeling about destroying the chapel, but had to carry out his commander's orders. Colonel Sanchez instructed his troops to begin tearing down the church. As the detail of men approached the walls with picks and hammers to fulfill their orders, they froze in fear as six ghostly entities materialized from the walls of the chapel.

The soldiers watched in horror as the "demons" slowly floated toward them waving flaming swords over their heads, while all the time issuing a warning: *Do not touch the walls of this scared place.* Colonel Sanchez and his men dropped their tools and ran away screaming, never to return.

When Colonel Sanchez's commanding officer heard what took place, he returned to the Alamo himself with troops and a cannon. The general instructed his gunners to aim the cannon at the chapel and blow it to pieces. Before the gunnery soldiers could prepare the cannon to fire, the ghostly monks reappeared with fiery swords in hand. As the phantoms approached, the general was on his horse and ready to give the order to fire. The ghosts startled his horse and the general was thrown into the air.

When he regained control over his horse, the general once again called for his men to fire. Wondering why his orders were not carried out, he looked back to see his men fleeing for their lives.

To his horror, he watched as a wall of flame erupted from the ground around the chapel. The smoke from the unholy fire then took the form of a large, imposing man. In each of the massive figure's hands were balls of fire, which he hurled at the general.

The general quickly rode away from the scene before the fireballs could hit him. When Santa Anna heard of the experiences of his most trusted officers, he ordered that the chapel not be touched. The Mexican soldiers and people of San Antonio believed the giant apparition was the collection of all the spirits of the men who died at the Alamo.

What was described could possibly be a spirit of smoke and fire, in other words a djinni. Djinn are noted for hanging around locations that have experienced great human suffering. This would include battlefields and locations of natural disasters. Islamic clerics believe certain types of djinn feed off the psychic energy left over from traumatic events.

The story above is a legend told by Alamo staff during a large group tour. There are no official documents that support the engrossing story of the Mexican soldiers' encounter with the six phantom monks or the giant being made of smoke. The evidence suggests that the Mexican soldiers did successfully level many of the walls of the fort and dismantle the wooden palisade that had been built in front of the church and along the south wall of the compound.

Between 1890 and 1896, the ghostly activity at the Alamo was big news in San Antonio. In 1894 the city used the chapel as a police headquarters and jail. It was not long before prisoners housed in the old barracks started to complain about all kinds of ghostly activity that took place in the night.[28]

The prisoners in the jail told detailed stories of a ghostly sentry who walked from east to west on the roof of the police station. They also said almost every night they saw apparitions running through the building as if being chased. The ghostly manifestations also included mysterious shadows and moaning sounds. The paranormal disturbances became so frequent that the guards and watchmen refused to patrol the building after hours.

The reports caused quite a stir with the governing board of San Antonio. Since no lawmen would work at the Alamo at night, the town council abandoned the old mission as a jail and looked for a new place to house prisoners.

The same paranormal incidents reported in 1894 have also been witnessed today. Several recent encounters tell of a phantom sentry that has been observed pacing quickly back and forth across the top of the Alamo. In addition to the presence of the ghostly sentry, tourists report seeing human-shaped forms along the walls of the Alamo chapel after dark. Sometimes the manifestations are accompanied by the disembodied screams of men.

Visitors at the Alamo insist that they have heard voices and whispers, as if the spirits of the dead were attempting to communicate with the world of the living. Some people

---

28. The *San Antonio Express* reported on these events in February 1894 and August 1897.

tell stories about seeing strange lights, feeling eerie cold spots, and hearing a multitude of unexplained noises. The cold spots are very real, since on a number of occasions I have experienced the phenomenon while walking through the chapel.

A member of park security at the Alamo saw a man dressed in clothes from the 1830s on the grounds walking toward the library. As the guard hurried after the man, he observed that the he was wearing boots, a tall hat, and a long overcoat. To the ranger's surprise, the puzzling man faded away as he approached the chapel. Other security personnel have allegedly claimed to have seen the same apparition numerous times in the courtyard of the Alamo, both during the day and at night.

The most frequent ghost sighting is of a little boy who is said to haunt the gift shop. Visitors, employees, and park rangers claim to have seen a blond-haired boy of about twelve peering out into the courtyard from one of the store's high windows. The small boy is only visible from the waist up. Rangers who have searched the gift shop in hopes of catching the ghostly prankster have come up empty handed. In each instance they have concluded that there is no way that a real person could perch themselves in the window without something to climb up on. The gift shop is not part of the original structure and was built in 1930.

There is a story that during the last days of the Alamo, a small boy was evacuated from the mission. It is believed that this child returns to the same spot where he remembered seeing a loved one alive for the last time.

DAVY CROCKETT'S LAST STAND

The most famous person to die defending the Alamo was Davy Crockett. Crockett's part in the great battle was made famous by actor John Wayne in the big-budget movie *The Alamo*.[29] Today, people would like to believe Davy Crockett went down fighting, taking as many of the enemy as possible with him. This is what is portrayed in the movie. After all, Crockett was played by John Wayne, another American hero, who had considerable influence on the script and would not have it any other way. However, there is considerable disagreement on how dramatic Crockett's death was at the Alamo.

During my first visit I was shown two documents. The first was a list from a scribe who served under Santa Anna indicating that Crockett was one of five men who surrendered and was later shot. The other document was written by a servant by the name of "Joe" who survived the final siege. Joe stated that Crockett was one of the last to die, and that his body was found in a back room of the mission surrounded by the bodies of about twenty Mexican soldiers he had killed.

---

29. *The Alamo* is a 1960 film starring John Wayne as Davy Crockett, Richard Widmark as Jim Bowie, and Laurence Harvey as William B. Travis. It is rumored that John Wayne became obsessed with playing Davy Crockett; Wayne spent a great deal of his own money to make sure the script and scenery were historically accurate. According to one Hollywood story, during the filming Wayne was visited by the ghost of Crockett, who told Wayne what really took place. After John Wayne's death in 1979, people reported seeing Wayne's own spirit wandering the grounds of the Alamo.

If you ask most people what happened to Crockett's body, they will tell you that he was buried at the Alamo. Although there is a memorial for him and the men who died with him, no remains have ever been found. It is said Crockett is buried at the San Fernando Cathedral in San Antonio, but no one really knows. Most Texas historians and Alamo experts believe Crockett's body was burned with the rest of the defenders. Is it possible the spirit of the great American is not at rest and wanders the grounds of the Alamo with many of his companions?

CROCKETT'S RESTLESS SPIRIT

During March each year, park rangers have observed a transparent figure, dressed in buckskin clothing and a coonskin hat, carrying a flintlock rifle and standing guard near the chapel. This is believed to be the spirit of none other than Davy Crockett himself. One of most terrible phantom images to play out at the old mission occurs in the Long Barracks. The ghostly scenario replays the way Crockett supposedly died.

One night a ranger on patrol entered the barracks and observed a man leaning against the wall. He was wearing buckskin clothing typically worn by frontiersmen during the 1800s. To the ranger it appeared the man's upper chest had been riddled with bullet holes. Then, before the ranger could react, several Mexican soldiers stepped from the darkness and encircled the stranger with bayonets mounted on their rifles. The ghostly soldiers pounced on the man, thrusting their long blades through his body.

The ranger said he would never forget the look on the man's face—it was a look of anguish and pain. In an instant the ethereal apparitions just faded away. The ranger was so frightened at what he witnessed that it took him several minutes to regain his composure and run out of the room.

MY INVESTIGATION IN 1975

A friend of mine, who at the time was a member of Alamo park security, gave me a special tour. He also told me he and other guards, as well as many staff members and tourists, had seen ghostlike apparitions appear on the grounds during the day and night.

Reports of ghostly activity have also been reported by guests at nearby hotels. On many occasions since the first report in 1956, people in hotel rooms that face the Alamo have reported seeing horrible apparitions coming out of the walls of the Alamo.

The phantoms were in the form of men who appeared to be bloody from battle. Some witnesses reported they saw the defenders of the Alamo walking back and forth on top of the buildings as if on guard duty. All of the sightings were reported between two and three in the morning.

On June 21, 1975, over thirty people staying at the Emily Morgan hotel, which is just across the street from the Alamo, reported hearing the sounds of screams, explosions, and trumpets blowing.

My contact told me a number of officers had quit their jobs after seeing "wandering" apparitions during the night on the lawn and in the old cemetery. The phantoms were reported to be moaning and crying as they walked across the grass. The officers who saw them reported that they looked "as solid as you or me, but were able to walk through the walls."

One of the most frequently seen apparitions appears in the garden. The ghost appears dripping wet, as if it had just ridden a long distance in the pouring rain. Many of the staff members who have seen the ghost speculate the spirit may have been one of the twenty riders that Alamo commander William Travis sent to Sam Houston seeking assistance.

Another phantom that makes his presence known is thought to be an Alamo defender. He has been seen by countless visitors and staff members during the day, poking his head and shoulders out of the large rectangular window over the double doors at the front of the mission. After leaning out and apparently looking around, he leans back and disappears. Another apparition frequently seen is that of a woman who appears next to the well in the back of the mission. She is seen only at night and is surrounded by a thick white vapor.

After walking with me around the outside of the Alamo and telling me a multitude of ghost stories, my friend asked if I would like to see the lower level. Of course I said yes, since I'd heard that many of the apparitions had appeared in that area.

As we walked to the back and down a number of steps, I was told the space was used for storage and nobody would come down alone. It seems there had been reports of the spirit of a tall Native American following people around or standing silently in the darkness. A second or so after the witness looks directly at him, the apparition vanishes.

According to historical documents displayed at the Alamo, an unknown number of Native Americans served as scouts. It is also on record that somewhere between two and five of them died in the siege of the Alamo.

I must admit: it was a very spooky place, and I could understand why anyone coming down alone and spending time there would get the jitters. Unfortunately, that day the Indian ghost did not make an appearance. I spent the rest of the day interviewing staff members who had encounters with the spirits who haunt the Alamo.

Several historians and members of the maintenance crew told me they had seen a Mexican officer slowly walking the grounds and inside the buildings. One janitor got close enough to see his uniform had the rank of general. This leads many to believe the ghost is General Manuel Fernández Castrillón, who was a commander in Santa Anna's infantry. Castrillón was one of the few high-ranking officers who were against the execution of the survivors of the Alamo after they surrendered. He gave the brave defenders his word that if they put down their arms, he would petition Santa Anna to let them live. However, Santa Anna said no and ordered the men to be hacked with sabers until they were dead. Could it be the honorable Castrillón's spirit is not at rest because he felt guilty about not being able to keep his word?

There have also been sightings of a tall man and a young child standing on the roof of the Alamo just before sunrise.

According to framed documents at the Alamo library, a Colonel Juan Andrade of the Mexican army stated in the final hours of the siege he saw a man with a small child in his arms leap to the ground at the rear of the Alamo church. Both died on impact. The colonel went on to say he was both horrified and saddened by the sight.

The ghosts of two boys are also seen following large tour groups. According to reports, the boys just "appear" behind the group, follow for a while, and then vanish. Since a number of people got a good look at the boys, they were able to describe them in detail. They are thought to be the nine- and eleven-year-old sons of Alamo defender Anthony Wolfe. According to Alamo library documents, the boys were killed in the final assault. Hiding in the Alamo Mission, they were mistaken for Alamo defenders and killed by the Mexican infantry.

I have no doubt, nor do hundreds of other people, that the Alamo and the surrounding area is extremely haunted. Tourists, rangers, and other staff continue to hear the screams and see the ghosts of those who died in the battle. Other phenomena that also occur include eerie cold spots throughout the buildings, vanishing lights, and unexplained noises. During my many visits in the mid-1970s I experienced these cold spots a number of times while walking through the hallowed halls and rooms of the Alamo.

MY 1984 VISIT

In 1984 I was asked, along with Dr. J. Allen Hynek, to make a presentation at the annual UFO conference of the Mutual

UFO Network (MUFON). As the hotel where I was staying was very close to downtown San Antonio, I decided to spend at least one day visiting the Alamo to see if there were any new sightings or other types of paranormal activity.

I arrived at the Alamo on a Saturday afternoon and was disappointed to find out that all the people I'd met nine years previously, including my contact, were no longer there. I spend the day going through some material and talking with a number of people. The staff seemed quite reluctant to discuss ghost sightings and other unusual activity. A tour guide confided in me, saying that the sightings had been escalating over the years and the "people in charge" wanted to play the hauntings down. I was able to collect several more staff encounters for my records, but they definitely were not as open to giving out information as they were in 1975.

As I walked around the grounds and into the chapel, the feelings of despair, dread, and sorrow seemed much greater than during my last visit almost ten years before. It was an interesting visit, since while walking through the mission and grounds, I actually saw several people crying. Was it possible on some unconscious level these people were picking up the remnants of the psychic signature left over after the thirteen days of glory at the siege of the Alamo?

Several years ago my brother relocated to Houston. I had never discussed my investigation and experiences at the Alamo with him. During the summer of 2009 he was visiting family in New York and Connecticut. I asked him if he and his wife had been to San Antonio to see the River Walk and the Alamo. He told me they loved the River Walk but got a very strange, uneasy feeling while walking through the Alamo and the surrounding gardens. I asked him if he could clarify "uneasy," and with a serious voice my brother said, "Sorrow." My brother has no interest or belief in the paranormal, yet he said, "If there was a place that was haunted, the Alamo was it."

As of 2011 paranormal investigation and ghost hunting are not allowed at the Alamo. The governing board and the city of San Antonio continue to play down the hauntings and strange occurrences. It is my personal feeling that due to the great number of reality shows on the paranormal, the people in charge of running the Alamo do not want an important historical event to be associated with so-called scientific investigators running around the Alamo at night trying to contact Davy Crockett.

CONCLUSION

If the horror of war, murders, and other terrible events can leave psychic imprints on the land and objects, then the Alamo definitely qualifies as one place that is extremely charged with psychic energy. Are the so-called ghosts reported at the Alamo really the restless spirits of the men who died there? Are they nothing more than mindless impressions left in the fabric of space and time, continuously playing out like some cosmic recording? The answers to these questions are not easy. Perhaps someday, when human beings have a better understanding of the universe, we will be able to solve the mystery of the hauntings at the Alamo.

CHAPTER 9

THE CURSE OF OWLSBURY

In 1993, *Ghostbusters* star Dan Aykroyd called this old ghost town "the most haunted place on earth."[30] No, he was not talking about the infamous witch trials in Salem, Massachusetts, or the home of the Headless Horseman in Sleepy Hollow, New York. He was referring to an almost forgotten ghost town called Dudleyville, or "Dudleytown" as it is sometimes known, located in northern Connecticut.

Dudleyville, originally called Owlsbury, is an abandoned eighteenth-century ghost town located in Litchfield County near Cornwall. The town and the land surrounding it are said to be cursed. Those who dare venture into its borders have reported sightings of ghosts, strange lights, bizarre demonic creatures, and even the devil himself.

Due to its haunted reputation, Dudleyville has attracted dozens of paranormal investigators and self-proclaimed "ghost

---

30. In an August 1993 interview in *Playboy* magazine.

hunters" for decades. This has resulted in the current landowners posting *No Trespassing* signs, which, by the way, are strictly enforced by local authorities. So unless you are willing to take the chance of getting a fine or even worse— arrested—then my advice would be to stay away unless you have written permission from the landowners.

THE CURSE

No one seems to know how the curse began. Some say it can be traced back to the early sixteenth century to an English nobleman, an ancestor of the first Dudleys who moved to Owlsbury. The legend says that an Edmund Dudley was executed for conspiring against King Henry VII. At his beheading a curse was placed on the entire family and their descendants by a bishop whose loyalty to the king was greater than his oath to God. According to the legend, the curse followed the descendants of Edmund Dudley into the new world.

From the late eighteenth through to the early twentieth century, many of the town's residents apparently became victims of the curse. There were reports of violent deaths, suicides, attacks by demonic monster-like creatures, and many hardships. Some say the town was built on Native American sacred ground, and powerful earth spirits took revenge on the settlers who built and farmed there, driving them out with fear and even death.

HISTORY

In 1738 Thomas Griffith bought a large parcel of land near Cornwall, Connecticut, and over several years built a town that he called Owlsbury because of the many creepy sounds they heard at night that early residents thought at first were screech and barn owls. As time went on, many more families moved into the small village and it began to grow. The first family with the last name of Dudley moved into Owlsbury in 1747, and in time many of their relatives also moved in. Because there were so many Dudleys now living in the town, it was known unofficially as Dudleyville or Dudleytown.

In 1748 Abiel Dudley went mad after claiming that he saw the devil appear in his home. Abiel lived to the ripe old age of ninety and, according to documents, died in his home. One year later a Nathan Carter and his family bought Abiel Dudley's home but moved out in a matter of weeks after seeing the ghost of Abiel in the house. The ghost often appeared to them late at night and would warn the family that unless they got out of town the devil would come and drag them into Hell.

In 1764 the new residents of the Abiel house, a couple and their five children, all died from cholera. One week after their death, villagers heard the screams of children in the night—and some claimed to have seen their spirits walking up and down the street and running into the woods as if playing.

In 1765 Aaron Oaken, a shepherd and Dudleyville resident, watched as the curse destroyed his entire family and livestock. Each day he would find at least one of his sheep "cut into pieces." He never did see the predator; it was as if it was invisible. He thought it was the work of the devil and cursed the fallen angel by challenging him to appear in front of him. Within a week of that challenge, his wife died of tuberculosis and his children wandered into the woods one day and disappeared. No traces of the children were ever found. One month later his house burned down. According to the story, one early evening Oaken walked into the woods as if in a hypnotic trance and was never seen again.

In 1792 Gerson Hollister, a resident of the town, went mad after claiming to have met the devil while tending to his sheep in a nearby pasture. Hollister claimed that he discovered a demon sucking the blood from his animals. He said the demon looked at him with "swirling red eyes," resulting in him going mad. Shortly after, Hollister was found dead; his body had multiple lacerations and bites as if it had been attacked by an animal.

Also in 1792 William Tanner went insane, claiming to have seen the devil. Tanner claimed that Hollister was attacked by a demonic animal with thick black fur, large claws, and fangs. Within a short time after his encounter, Tanner died of unknown causes. Tanner was known as a recluse who lived on the outskirts of town. Some Dudleyville residents believed that Tanner murdered Hollister, but there was never any proof that he was guilty of the dastardly crime.

A neighbor of Hollister's was skeptical of the story and said she did not believe in the devil. The next day she was killed after having been struck by lightning with no thunder while walking through the street on a clear, sunny day.

The famous newspaper editor and (later) presidential candidate Horace Greeley married Dudleyville native Mary Cheney in 1836. A week before the 1872 presidential election, in which her husband was a candidate, she hanged herself for no apparent reason. Some historians of Dudleyville say that Mary Cheney was depressed and often talked of suicide, but there are no documents to prove one way or the other what her state of mind was before she took her life. Although Greeley married a Dudleyville woman, there is no evidence that he ever lived in the village or even visited it.

Many people who lived in the village with the last name of Dudley died a horrific death. Some went insane and committed suicide. Others were found "hacked to pieces" from what some say is a mysterious beast that lives in the forest, while others think they were killed by "wild Indians."

The farms in Dudleyville began to fail in 1892. This is still a mystery today, since the land should have been ideal for farming and raising livestock. Plants and animals died for no apparent cause. Some historical accounts say that dogs, cows, and horses were found in the fields mutilated by some unknown assailant or predator.

In 1892 John Brophy and his family moved into Dudleyville hoping to start a new life and do some farming. Within one week, his wife mysteriously died and two of his children disappeared without a trace. In 1901 residents reported finding the tracks of "hoofed demons" that appeared in the night and killed their sheep. John Brophy himself was found with his clothes torn and deep scratches in his body. He claimed that the devil attacked him and told him that unless he and everybody in the town left, demonic spirits would rise out of Hell and kill them all. While recovering in his home, Brophy disappeared one night and was never seen again.

Finally, in 1937 a Dr. William Clark came home one day to find his wife muttering insanely about the devil. In the days to follow she went completely mad and had to be committed to an asylum for the insane. Dr. Clark remained in the town for a while, but moved out within two months because of "strange sights and sounds at night." Shortly after 1937 Dudleyville lost its remaining residents and became a ghost town.

Before he moved out of Dudleyville, Dr. Clark founded Dark Entry Forest, Inc., an association of property owners in the area that designated Dudleyville as a nature preserve. Over the years the forest has reclaimed what once was the town, and all that is left are stone foundations and a few walls.

DUDLEYVILLE TODAY

In modern times there are many stories about people seeing ghosts that they believe are the former residents of the town walking through the woods and entering the foundations that used to be their homes. Hikers have claimed to hear the cries of disembodied spirits trying to find their way to the next world. People who dare enter through the forest path to Dudleyville called "Dark Entrance" claim to hear the screams of some type of creature that is neither human nor animal.

On one occasion several people reported seeing a number of pentagrams on the ground, then hearing a loud, deep voice telling them to get out. In the summer of 1995 paranormal thrill-seekers walking through the ghost town claimed to have seen a large hairy creature running through the woods. People who have visited the area or drive by in their cars claim to feel uneasy, while some feel nauseous or develop a spontaneous heavy feeling or pain in their head.

Before the current landowners restricted access to the ghost town, I visited Dudleyville a number of times and also experienced a very uneasy feeling. As you walk along the dirt path that leads to where the town once was stood, there are no sounds of birds or any wildlife—only dead silence.

The last time I walked through the ghost town was in 1989. I parked my car and began my slow progression through the woods, keeping my eyes and ears open to the slightest movement or sound. The most eerie thing about my visit was the silence; it was very quiet, like death. Despite it being a beautiful July morning, there were no birds chirping, no squirrels running in the woods or up the trees, and no sounds of nearby civilization. As I looked up to the clear blue sky I noticed no birds flying overhead, even at high altitude. It was apparent that animals avoided the place.

I also found this to be the case with the stone chambers in New York's Hudson River Valley. The chambers are also the scene of a multitude of reported paranormal phenomena. I have documented the existence of magnetic anomalies in and around many of them. Wild animals stay out of the chambers and dogs being walked on a leash refuse to enter, despite the encouragement of their masters. The only animal found in one of the stone chambers was a barn swallow. For some reason this bird prefers to make a nest on the chamber wall that is always aligned with north.

I thought to myself, *Perhaps the land is located under a very intense magnetic anomaly, and this is why animals stay away.* Scientists in the United States and Europe have discovered that magnetic fields do affect animals and people to various degrees. Just how the magnetic field acts on a living organism depends on its species and age. For example, it was found that certain fish and birds have small amounts of magnetite in their brains. Magnetite is a highly magnetic form of iron and pulls on the tissue, creating electrical impulses when exposed to a negative or positive magnetic anomaly.

There is also some research to indicate that intense magnetic fields can produce bizarre behavior in humans, as well as hallucinations or visions. We do know for sure that magnetic fields affect animals. The next time you are at a farm, take a look at the cows. Bizarre as it may seem, cows don't stand around randomly chewing in the field; they behave like huge compasses, aligning the front of their bodies with magnetic north. A recent study of thousands of high-resolution satellite images of pastures around the world discovered that all types of cattle did in fact align themselves with magnetic north while grazing. Why they do this is a mystery to not only the biologist but also the physical scientist.

Finally, as I mention in my book *Interdimensional Universe*, psychics seem to be sensitive to changes in magnetic fields. During my research on the stone chambers, a well-known psychic who lives in Danbury, Connecticut, was able to point out the location of the anomalies at several locations weeks before I did my investigations with a research-grade magnetometer. Is it possible that a strong magnetic anomaly at Dudleyville has such a powerful influence on the human mind to create some type of misinterpretation of natural events? Perhaps someday in the future, if the owners of the land once again open the area to the public, I will be able to bring my equipment there and conduct a detailed investigation.

MEANWHILE, BACK AT DUDLEYVILLE

When I visited Dudleyville in 1989, I took out my hand compass and noticed a fourteen-degree deviation at the beginning of the trail that led to the village. The highest deviation of eighteen degrees from north was obtained in what was once the center of town. Although this indicated a magnetic anomaly, in my opinion it was not enough to cause the human brain to induce visions of strange blood-drinking creatures or the devil, or to result in murders and suicides.

It must be considered that using a compass is not conclusive to determine the extent and type of a magnetic anomaly. It is my desire to bring in an array of scientific instruments, including a magnetometer, to Dudleyville. However, due to strict trespassing restrictions by the current landowners, this will not possible in the foreseeable future.

I continued to walk the dirt path and came to an area that was outlined by large oval stones. It looked as if someone was trying to mark a location. Could it have been a warning alerting people not to walk beyond that point, or were they markers indicating the location of several hidden gravesites?

According to town records in Hartford, there was no cemetery at Dudleyville and the departed were taken to a burial site in the town of Cornwall. It was obvious someone went through a great deal of trouble to carve the stones in a conical shape and place them in the ground. I estimated that each stone must have weighed anywhere from 1,200 to 1,800 pounds. What was even more puzzling was they all were made up of a metamorphic rock called gneiss. Gneiss is common to the area and produced when granite is subjected to great heat and pressure over a long period of time.

During my time at Dudleyville, which was a little over two hours, I only had one thing on my mind—and that was to get out as soon as possible. There was a feeling of heaviness in the air, and depression, which seemed to penetrate into the very core of my being.

As I was walking down the trail back to my car, I noticed a person coming in my direction. It was a woman, perhaps in her late twenties. She stopped to say hi and we talked a while about how creepy the place is. The story she told me appears below, and I feel it is worth being included in this chapter. I can't remember her name, but I was able to tape her on my trusty cassette recorder.

The recorded information has been sitting in my files since 1989. I only listened to it once before, in early 1990.

Recently I wiped the dust off the case and began to listen again. I was amazed on how much the case supports my work into the theory that most paranormal phenomena are the result of alternate dimensions interacting with our own. Here is the woman's story:

"It was in 1983, late in the summer, when I had the experience in Dudleyville. I parked my car and walked down the trail that leads to the old ghost town. I had gone there several times before, since there were all kinds of stories about supernatural things going on. I wanted to see if it was all real, but until that day I never saw anything. The spooky thing about this place is, despite the woods, you really don't hear a sound. It's like all the animals stay away from the place. Animals can sense evil, and from what I understand of its history this place would rank number one.

"Anyway, I am walking down the trail and come to the village. It's in the middle of the day when I hear what sounded like thunder. I looked up to the sky, and there wasn't a cloud to be seen. Then I notice two children running down the opposite side of the trail into what was once the village square. They ran into one of the foundations and just vanished. Then I heard this sound coming from the woods. At first it sounded like a bear, but then its pitch changed and it sounded like a screech. It got louder. I stood there transfixed, staring into the woods waiting for something to come out. The thick brush was being pushed away and something heavy was snapping twigs on the ground. I was too afraid to move. I could actually see the bushes being pushed aside by this thing, but I could not see it. Whatever it was, the thing was invisible.

"Then the noise stopped, and I figured the creature saw me and was motionless looking at me. I turned around and ran back to my car. I didn't look back. But I knew something was running after me because I heard its footsteps. When I reached the end of the trail where my car was parked, the sound stopped. I got into my car and drove home. It has taken me over a year to get up the courage to come back."

We walked around for a while, and I was shown the location where she saw the "ghost" of the two boys and heard the creature. I took a number of pictures with my 35-mm-film camera. When the prints and negatives finally came back two weeks later from the film-processing laboratory, I was surprised to see several orbs of light on two frames around the location in the woods where she heard the noise.

Are Dudleyville and the woods surrounding it really haunted? Well, I guess we will never find out, since the location where the town once existed is closed to the public. In 1999 the current owners, Dark Entry Forest, even shut down the hiking trails. Many believe that the area was closed because of all the curious people visiting trying to see if the curse was real. Some say the area was closed off because there are strange things going on that the landowners are well aware of and want to keep secret.

Despite the area being closed off, a number of people who know about the reputation of the haunted ghost town have taken their chances and ventured into the woods. Some have been caught by the state police and fined for trespassing, while others seemingly got away with it.

Over the years I have collected thirty-four accounts from people who say they encountered an "invisible" creature in the woods. Some claim to have seen a large, hairy, wolf-like beast with long, thick, black fur; red eyes; and long canine fangs. Some brave hikers say they have seen a Bigfoot-like creature walking through the wooded area near the foundations of the old town. There are also reports of shadow-like entities walking in and out of the old foundations and woods.

In conclusion, no matter how skeptical you are, the historical accounts and encounters with the paranormal at Dudleyville speak for themselves. Most of these reports are well documented and have become part of the shadowy folklore of the state of Connecticut.

CHAPTER 10

OUT OF TIME AND PLACE

Is it really possible to travel back and forth in time? Although time travel continues to show up in the equations of theoretical physics, most scientists throw up a red flag when they appear. If you were able to travel back in time, is it possible you could meet yourself and give information or advice to your past self? If this information is used to change important decisions, then the future timeline will be altered, and this might be very dangerous.

One theory is that timelines are in constant flux, but we have no knowledge of it. For example, imagine you are good friends with your neighbor and have known this person for years. The pivotal point in the past is the decision of this neighbor to move next door to you. Let's say this person, for whatever reason, changes her mind in the past and decides not to buy the home next door to yours. The timeline now has changed, and you have a different neighbor. You never knew this other person, and he is not your friend. Although the timeline has changed, you have no awareness of anything being wrong.

There are several psychics I have come across during past years who claim they are able to "sense" the changes in timelines. When these take place, they "feel something is not right."

PARADOX

The *grandfather paradox* is a paradox of time travel first described by the science fiction writer René Barjavel in his 1943 book *The Imprudent Traveler*. Imagine a man traveling back in time and killing his biological grandfather before he ever met the time traveler's grandmother. What would be the obvious result? One of the time traveler's parents would never have been born, and therefore the time traveler himself would never have been conceived. Since the time traveler was never born, he could not have journeyed back in time to kill his grandfather.

Now it gets really strange. Since the grandfather did not die, the time traveler *was* conceived, allowing him to travel back in time and kill his grandfather. However, if he once again kills his grandfather, he could never be born to travel back in time and perform the deed. In this case a time loop is formed, and all parties involved continue to repeat the same day, week, month, or year over and over again. This time-loop paradox is illustrated in the movie *Groundhog Day*, starring Bill Murray.

The grandfather paradox has been used to argue that traveling back in time must be impossible. However, two theories have been proposed to avoid the paradox. The first simply states that events in the past are unchangeable, and no matter what the time traveler does, his grandfather still survives. The second theory is that the time traveler does kill his grandfather and does not change the future, but he creates an alternate reality with a different timeline. In one reality, the grandfather is dead and the traveler was never born. In the other reality, both the grandfather and the traveler are still alive.

Is it possible the past, present, and future or different alternate realities could merge together for a brief moment in time? There are quite a few theoretical physicists from major universities who do believe time travel is possible.[31] The concept of time is based on movement of celestial objects. Our clocks and calendars are based on the rotation of Earth and its revolution around the sun. There is also another type of movement, which goes unnoticed, that starts at the quantum level and expands to the largest clusters of galaxies.

For example, we know the universe is increasing in speed and expanding rapidly. With each nanosecond, our planet, solar system, and galaxy move forward in space and time. With each second, every molecule in our galaxy and our

---

31. See Stephen Hawking, Kip Thorne, Igor Novikov, Timothy Ferris, and Alan Lightman, *The Future of Spacetime* (Norton, 2002).

bodies is increasing in vibration to keep up with this movement. This is called *quantum signature*, and it identifies what time and part of the universe matter belongs to. With every nanosecond, everything around us, including our bodies, is in a different place and at a different vibrational level. If, for some reason, the atoms that make up your body did not stay in synchronization, then everything around you would disappear. You might be in a limbo-like existence in the space-time continuum.

Perhaps it is possible for the past and future, as well as alternate realities, to occasionally merge together. This could explain why there are so many "ghost sightings" and reports of creatures and people who seem out of time and place. I would like the dedicated "ghost hunters" to consider the following: perhaps sightings of phantom people dressed in clothes from hundreds of years ago are not sightings of ghosts, but of real people living in the past. If the past can merge with the present, we may able to see people who lived in a house long ago.

Most of the time it seems the awareness of perception is one way, but it may be possible for people from the past and present to actually see each other and communicate for an undetermined period of time. If this theory is even partially correct, then perhaps someone in the past or future may see a person in our present and think they are some strange apparition.

During my investigations of the paranormal, I have come across a number of cases in which different time periods seemed to have merged, allowing both subjects to view each other. Several of these cases are documented in my previous books *Files from the Edge* and *Interdimensional Universe*.

STRANGE PEOPLE

One of the most perplexing aspects of the study of the paranormal is people who appear to be out of time and place. One day they are reported in one area, are noticed for a length of time (which may be several days or years), and then vanish. For the most part they are considered strange-looking vagabonds who wander the countryside as if searching for something. They are usually dressed in out-of-style clothes or in some type of bizarre outfit that humans on Planet Earth never wore. In most cases they appear human but do not seem to understand any language. Is it possible these strange people could be from another time, reality, or dimension? UFO investigators who get involved in a case like this often think these people are really aliens stranded on Earth.

From 1983 until 1986, while investigating UFO and paranormal activity in the Hudson Valley area of New York, I came across reports of "strange people" being seen in the UFO hot spots. In some cases these strange people contacted witnesses who had encounters with the Hudson Valley UFOs. There would always be three of them, and they would come to the homes of the witnesses at all hours of the day and night. In one incident they showed up at six a.m. on a Sunday at a family home and did not seem to understand why their visit upset the people living there.

All three were described as being "male" and under six feet tall, with jet-black hair, pale white skin, and wearing sunglasses. Some of the more bizarre reports from witnesses indicated that the "men" seemed to be wearing lipstick and makeup on their faces. They all spoke in a monotone voice as if programmed and would not eat any food or drink any beverage. The people that contacted me who claimed an encounter with the three men said they were frightened by the visit. They were afraid to ask them to leave, because one of the men said they were from a "secret agency in the government of the United States that investigates sightings of UFOs and encounters with aliens." Please remember that these encounters took place many years before the popular *Men in Black* (MIB) movies.

It's interesting to note that all the witnesses who were visited by the strange men in black had a close encounter with the Hudson Valley UFO and were engulfed in a brilliant beam of white light. Many of the people who experienced this said it felt as if they were being "probed."

During their visit, the three "men" never sat down or relaxed and continued to ask questions for a time period from thirty to sixty minutes. When they left the homes of the witnesses, the "men" did not get into a car but walked away until they were gone.

There were thousands of witnesses who saw the Hudson Valley UFO. I really can't say how many were visited by the three strange men. During the 1980s I was contacted by eight families who said they had visits from the three men in black. All eight accounts are exactly the same, and from what I gather the questions the men asked the witnesses were the same or similar. In UFO circles, this type of experience would be classified as an "MIB" encounter.

JUST WHO ARE THE MEN IN BLACK?

The men in black (MIB) are a bizarre part of the UFO experience. They are always reported as being men in their late forties dressed in dark suits who claim to be government agents. They have been known to harass or even threaten UFO witnesses to keep them from talking about what they saw. They also have been reported to be very aggressive in keeping people who had a close encounter or a contact experience silent. In many cases they just ask the witnesses a number of questions and leave. It is thought by some UFO researchers that the MIB are aliens sent to check out people for a possible abduction or contact experiences.

Early reports of MIB date back to the early 1950s, and they were often described as being short in stature with pale and sometimes dark complexions. Men in black always seem to have detailed information on the people they contact, as if the individual had been under surveillance for a long period of time. They also have knowledge of where the witnesses saw the UFO and details of its sighting.

Although MIB were frequently reported in the 1950s and 1960s, some researchers like the late John Keel suggest the men in black are a modern-day manifestation of the same phenomena that were earlier interpreted as encounters with demons and fairies.[32] Keel was also the first to propose the idea that much of what we call the paranormal, including the MIB, originates from another dimensional reality.

John was a very good friend of mine, and his ideas influenced the direction of my research into not only UFOs but also all types of paranormal phenomena. Whoever or whatever the MIB are, they have become part of modern-day literature and folklore. Encounters with these strange beings have not only influenced the way we think about UFOs, but they have also influenced the movie industry.

THE STRANGE CASE OF KASPAR HAUSER

Kaspar Hauser was a young teenage boy who in 1828 appeared on the streets of Nürnberg, Germany. He was confused, unintelligible, and dressed in unusual clothes. He was taken off the streets by the local constable and questioned. The boy could not answer; it was as if he didn't understand the language. Also, he acted as if he was in a place that was not familiar to him.

After a lengthy examination by several doctors, it was determined the boy was not mentally ill. Having no name, the local authorities called him Kaspar Hauser. Kaspar was then placed in isolation without any human contact for an unknown period of time. For some reason the authorities did not want Kaspar to mingle with the populace. During his incarceration Kaspar proved to be very intelligent and was taught to read and write German within six months.

---

32. John Keel, *UFOs: Operation Trojan Horse* (Putnam, 1970).

However, despite being finally able to communicate, Kaspar could offer no explanation of who he was or where he was from. Kaspar would often say he was from a place that was dark and confined.

During experiments on the boy it was found that magnetic fields affected him in ways that were strange. When a Professor Daumer held the north pole of a magnet toward him, Kaspar put his hand on his stomach as if in pain. The south pole of the magnet seemed to have little or no effect.[33]

I found this account interesting, since I believe djinn are affected by magnetic fields. This may be also true even if they take human form. The djinn race are said to be made of "smokeless fire." In modern terminology this could be plasma. In physics and chemistry, plasma is a state of matter similar to gas in which a certain portion of the particles are ionized. Plasma is greatly affected by a magnetic field or an electromagnetic pulse. Such a being composed of mostly plasma could be harmed, killed, or contained using electromagnetic fields.

In Arabian folklore, the most powerful and evil djinn were imprisoned in bottles lined with a net of iron. Some were also held captive in crystalline rings of fire, opal, and quartz. Was Kaspar Hauser a djinni in human form? Of course this is pushing the evidence, but the report indicates that, like a djinni, his sensitivity to a magnetic field was much greater than that of a human being.

---

33. Anselm von Feuerbach, *Caspar Hauser*, translated by Gotfried Linberg (Allen and Ticknor, 1832), 132.

After three attempts on his life, Kaspar was moved to the town of Ansbach, where the town's judge placed him under protective custody. The historical record is not clear on who exactly tried to kill the boy, but makes it very apparent they were shot before they could do him harm.

Kaspar often said he was not from Germany, but somewhere else that was quite different. In 1833 Kaspar Hauser was stabbed to death by unknown assailants. From the first day of his mysterious appearance it seems that there was a group of people or a secret organization who wanted him dead.

Over the past 180 years there have been a number of speculations concerning the true identity of Kaspar Hauser. In 1996, a major German magazine did DNA tests of the blood on Hauser's clothes and could not find a match with any family in Germany. It seems the true identity of Kaspar Hauser will remain unknown until permission is obtained to open Hauser's grave and test his remains. This may never happen, because for some reason the German government will not allow it. Many feel the government is hiding something about the boy's true identity, but what?

Is it possible that Kaspar Hauser accidently walked through a portal from another parallel reality? Could this be the reason why he was isolated in the nineteenth century and forbidden to talk with anyone? Is this the real reason why the German government is still covering up today? We can only speculate, but Kaspar Hauser is one person who seemed out of place and time.

THE LEATHERMAN

People living in eastern Connecticut and the Hudson Valley of New York have heard the strange story of the Leatherman, but many of the younger generations and those living in other parts of the country have not. The Leatherman was a wandering "hobo" who traveled an endless 365-mile circle between towns in Connecticut and those located on the east side of the Hudson River in New York during the mid-to-late 1800s.

The strange man never spoke and would communicate his likes and dislikes with grunts or other gestures. He was called the Leatherman because the only clothes he wore were handmade stitched sections of leather that some estimate weighed over sixty pounds.

The Leatherman was first seen in Connecticut sometime around 1862 and looked so strange that all who encountered him wanted to know who he was. When confronted and questioned, he would only look at people with a perplexing expression on his face, then grunt and walk away. Some people in Connecticut and New York thought he was an angel who was testing their kindness and charity. Wanting to keep within the graces of God, several families in each town took it upon themselves to give him food and drink when he made his yearly appearance. The Leatherman would never accept work or money, and despite being heckled by children he never responded to them and just continued on his way.

During his long yearly trek, the Leatherman would live in rock shelters and caves that are known today. According to historical records he was often seen resting in the stone chambers of Westchester and Putnam counties in New York.

The towns on his endless journey included New Fairfield, Roxbury, New Milford, Thomaston, Middletown, and Danbury in Connecticut; and North Salem, Briarcliff Manor, Brewster, Patterson, Pawling, Peekskill, Putnam Valley, Tarrytown, and Mount Kisco in New York.

For almost thirty years the Leatherman made his journey through the blazing heat of summer and the frigid cold of winter. Like clockwork, each year he arrived in each town exactly one year later to the day. The Great Blizzard of 1888 was the only time his journey was delayed by three days. It was after this terrible winter that the famous Leatherman vanished.

WHERE DID HE GO?

As mysteriously as he appeared, the Leatherman disappeared. Historians believe the bitter cold and snow finally caught up with him. Some say he was found dead in a cave near Sing Sing, New York. Another story says the Leatherman was found unconscious in the snow with his hands and feet frozen. He was taken to a hospital in Hartford and placed in a private room. The next day when the nurses went to check on him, he could not be found. Just how he was able to escape the hospital without being seen remains a mystery to this day. Still another story found in the Derby, Connecticut, public library says he developed oral cancer and was found dead in one of the caves he frequented in March of 1889.

In its section for books about Connecticut history, the Derby library has one of the only pictures taken of the Leatherman. According to a document at the Derby library, he was buried in Sparta Cemetery, which is right off Route 9 in Scarborough, New York, only fifteen minutes from Sleepy Hollow.

In 1999 I traveled the path of the Leatherman with the hope of obtaining information about his true identity. At every town that was once his stop, the people in the historical societies and libraries had a different theory of who he was. During the summer months I also explored the rock shelters, caves, and stone chambers in Watertown, Connecticut, and Brewster, New York, where many believe the Leatherman would rest and seek shelter. I explored each location with the hope of finding a clue, but found nothing. While exploring the small caves I found it quite remarkable anyone could live in such a harsh environment for the better part of twenty-plus years!

During my visit to what is now called "Leatherman Cave" in Watertown, I met several people hiking. They told me on more than one occasion while photographing inside the cave they were able to pick up glowing spheres of light or orbs. They and many others believe the lights are the ghost of the Leatherman. Several days later they e-mailed me their photographs. After examining the images on my computer it was apparent the globes of light taken in the Leatherman Cave looked very similar to images of orbs taken in and around the stone chambers of New York.

According to one legend among the old-time residents of Brewster, one day in the summer of 1862 the Leatherman appeared out of a burst of light from one of the old stone chambers. This story is of considerable interest to me, since the stone chambers have been the scene of a number of paranormal experiences, including dozens of UFO sightings and close encounters with "alien beings." Native Americans of the Wappinger and Algonquin tribes also believe that they are "doorways" to another world.

During the summer of 2009 I was able to receive a great deal of electronic voice phenomena on a rapid-scan radio device. The EVP recorded during that year could possibly indicate these structures are the locations of dimensional portals. The majority of the communications indicated we were dealing with dimensional beings that identified themselves as "djinn." In some cases the communicating entity would say it was a human being in another reality trying to communicate with the dead.

According to local folklore in Putnam County, the Leatherman buried gold in one of the chambers that has never been found. This could be the reason why so many of these structures were destroyed or damaged during the late nineteenth and early twentieth centuries.

JUST WHO WAS THE LEATHERMAN?

In the summer of 1999 I tracked down the alleged burial spot of the Leatherman in Sparta Cemetery. His headstone was located no more than twenty feet from the road and read:

Final Resting Place of
Jules Bourglay

Of Lyons, France
"The Leather Man"

One of the many theories of the Leatherman's identity is that he was from France and his name was Jules Bourglay. However, according to genealogist, historian, and former educator Dan DeLuca, his identity is still unknown.[34] The name Jules Bourglay first appeared in a story published in the *Waterbury Daily American* on August 16, 1884. The story was later retracted on March 25, 1889, indicating there was no documentation to prove who the Leatherman really was. Also, there is no tangible evidence to prove the Leatherman is actually buried in Sparta Cemetery.

It has been speculated by local mystery hunters that the name and dates on the tombstone are actually a code giving the Leatherman's true identity and origin. The markings on his grave only add more mystery to the strange tale of the Leatherman.

Is it possible the Leatherman was from another reality and could not find his way back home? Perhaps he fell through a dimensional window and got lost in our world. The Leatherman would walk the same route year after year as if looking for something. Was he actually looking for another dimensional window to open up so he could once again return to his reality? No one can say for sure, but there is no doubt he was not just a legend, but a real person who was out of place—and time.

---

34. Dan W. DeLuca, *The Old Leather Man: Historical Accounts of a Connecticut and New York Legend* (Wesleyan University Press, 2008).

GHOST OR TIME TRAVELER?

The case presented below may not be a ghost story, but rather is one of those rare moments in which the past and present overlap. The case concerns a young man who was twenty-one in 1973, when he was challenged to spend the night in an old, abandoned mansion that once stood on the shore of Long Island Sound in a section of Rye, New York. Although the witness passed away in 2008, I will only refer to him using his first name, which was is Rick.

As a freshman attending a private university in southern New York State, Rick wanted to join a fraternity. As part of his hazing he was ordered to stay overnight in the old abandoned house mentioned above. According to local folklore the house is haunted by a very "scary ghost" with long black hair and a beard. The locals called the house "The Old Mansion," and children would often dare each other just to walk by it, but they would never enter through its doorway, which was surrounded by terrifying statues of gargoyles.

The mansion had thirty rooms with five acres of property, which was mostly woods. The exact date of construction is not known, but it was abandoned in 1933. It must have been quite beautiful in its day, since there were many gardens and its eastern side looked over the waters of Long Island Sound. The first time I saw the building was in the early 1960s, and I always thought it resembled the mansion in Edgar Allan Poe's story "The Fall of the House of Usher." The mansion was located far from the road, and because of this it gave visitors the feeling of isolation.

Looking at the timeworn building from the outside—with its decaying walls being invaded by creeping, strangulating vines and vacant dark windows—one gets the feeling this is the last place on Earth one would choose to be, especially at night. The structure had a presence to it, like something alive, watching and waiting for some foolish person to venture through its doorway into the inner sanctum. Those who were daring enough to enter never did so again. Rick was one of those people.

RICK'S NIGHT OF TERROR

Rick arrived at the old mansion at sunset on a day in late September. He had a flashlight, a blanket, a pillow, and some reading material. He figured it was going to be a long night, so he also brought along several bottles of beer. The front door was bolted shut, so he entered through a broken window in the basement. As Rick made his way upstairs he froze in his tracks. He heard a noise from the first level that sounded like human voices. It was clearly a man yelling, but he could not make out the words.

As Rick continued to listen he could also hear a woman and two children screaming something while crying. At first Rick thought that someone was in the house, perhaps the caretaker. If this was so he could get fined for trespassing and perhaps even arrested. Rick slowly made his way to the first level, and the voices stopped. The house was now dark; standing motionless and listening, he did not hear or see a living soul.

Rick then thought perhaps what he heard were ghosts, but he laughed at himself for even considering this explanation. He was a science major and firmly believed that ghosts, UFOs, and other things of the so-called world of the paranormal did not exist. It was his opinion at the time that otherworldly forces and creatures were nothing more than products of the overactive imaginations of unstable or bored people.

He prepared his camp next to a beautiful marble staircase that gently spiraled upward as it joined the main level with the second floor. Lying on his blanket with only a small flashlight as a source of illumination, he began to read. The darkness that surrounded his small light was silent. At times Rick would flash his light into the dark because he felt as if someone was standing motionless in the blackness staring at him.

After about an hour of reading Rick put the flashlight and book down and rubbed his eyes. Then a sound as if two doors slamming, one right after another, came from upstairs. The noise was so loud he jumped to his feet, grabbed the light, and ran to the landing of the stairs.

He looked up to the second floor and saw a glowing figure floating toward the top of the stairs. He stood frozen and was able to make out that the apparition was a man of about fifty wearing a gold robe with a pipe in his mouth and a book in his hand. The image was about to enter a door when it stopped, turned, and looked at Rick. In his own words, Rick related to me his story in a 1978 interview:

"I was scared and could not move. The guy was floating about a foot above the ground. I couldn't see his feet because there were all these wavy lines. He was radiating a soft white light that surrounded his entire body. We just stood there staring at each other. It was only a few seconds, but it seemed like forever. The ghost, or whatever you want to call it, while still looking at me gasped as if frightened, and the pipe fell from his mouth and disappeared before it hit the floor. I think this ghost was actually surprised to see me and was scared out of his mind. The ghost jumped right through the closed door and vanished. I then heard all of these voices coming from the room, but couldn't make out what they were saying. It sounded like several men and women talking really fast. I was scared and finally got the courage to turn around and run. I was on the first floor in what could have been the living room, which had large windows. I broke the glass with my flashlight and climbed out. I ran to my car never looking back, and took off and never returned."

A BIZARRE TWIST

I was aware of the strange happenings in the "Old Mansion" for many years before my interview with Rick. You see, back in the early 1960s I was one of the kids who would walk past the place on a dare. The legends of the place were well known in the Rye-Port Chester area of New York. According to a 1933 story in the *Port Chester Daily Item*, the original family who lived there moved out because of paranormal activity.[35] They claimed to have seen a hideous-looking, demonic ghost with a long, black beard and long hair wearing "strange" clothes. In 1973 Rick actually had long hair with a black, thick beard. At the time he went into the house he was wearing jeans with a tie-dye shirt. This style of clothes and hair was common in the late 1960s and early 1970s, but would have been considered utterly strange and weird in the 1930s.

Is it possible this was a case when the past was able to view the present? Perhaps the man at the top of the stairs was not a ghost, but a real person going about his business in his home in the early twentieth century. The man seemed surprised with fear to see Rick, who in turn was startled to see the man. Could it be each person in their respective time periods thought the other one was a ghost?

To someone in the early part of the twentieth century, Rick would have been a scary sight with his long hair and beard. Is it possible the demonic ghost reported by the family who lived in the house in the early 1930s was actually Rick? When I finally put all the pieces together it sounded like an episode from *The Twilight Zone*. The story above is true and, as Rod Serling would say, it is "submitted for your approval."

---

35. H. B. Meltzer, "Ghosts Chase Family out of Their Home," *The Port Chester Daily Item*, June 19, 1933.

WAS IT TIME TRAVEL OR JUST A DREAM?

The account below is perhaps one of the most bizarre cases in my files. It has to do with a person who believes that he traveled back in time to attempt to give advice to himself as a child. The story is unique since there are a number of interesting points that I have never heard before. Below is a transcript from a 1998 interview I did with the person who made this incredible claim:

"I have to start from the beginning to tell you this incredible story. It's hard to accept, but as an adult I traveled back in time and saw myself as a child. I was ten years old and lived in a large apartment building in New York City. There were lots of kids, and we often played in the building. One of our games we all loved to play was 'Monster.' In this game one of the kids would wear a mask and pretend to be a monster on the loose. We would all have toy guns and pretend to be the army and police trying to track the monster down and kill it.

"It was an evening in August and a there was a severe thunderstorm, but we still played the game even though most of us were afraid of the thunder and lightning. We were all excited since it made the game even scarier. One of the kids dressed up like the wolf man and went up the stairs as we waited in the lobby. After ten minutes we would go and track him down—shoot the monster and destroy it. If he caught us alone or by surprise, he would kill us. The apartment complex was very large. It had fifteen floors with a back staircase and a front staircase with a great number of hallways and plenty of places to hide.

"The storm raged on as we played our game, and then the lights went out and all of us were left in darkness. One of the kids lived on the first floor, and he was able to make his way to his apartment and got several flashlights. I was given one, and we all continued with the game to find the monster and destroy it. I was separated from the group, but continued my search. I went up to the fifteenth floor and heard a banging sound coming from the next level, which was the floor where the roof door was. I turned the corner of the staircase and looked up and saw this man standing there. The door was swinging open and shut from the wind, and the flashes of lightning made him look like some type of ghostly apparition.

"I was scared out of my wits because this man was trying to talk and waving his hands gesturing me to come up. There was something familiar about him, but I was too scared and ran downstairs to the lobby. When I got down to the lobby all my friends were there. They told me they quit playing because things got 'freaky.' What they meant by this I never found out; perhaps some of them also had some type of experience. I told them about the man on the roof floor, and we all bravely went back up. The roof door was open, but nobody was there. I went to my apartment for dinner and told my parents about the man. My father said it must have been some 'bum' trying to get out of the storm. Now comes the strangest part of this story.

"Last year I turned fifty on August 22, and on my birthday there was a severe thunderstorm. Having been divorced for several years I was alone and just decided to spend my birthday watching television alone. During the storm the power went out. I was in bed and went to sleep. In a dream-like state I felt myself drifting, and there was this bright light and all of a sudden I was sucked into a long, dark spiral tunnel. I then was on a floor with a staircase below. There was a boy at the bottom, whom I recognized as me when I was ten. I thought it would be great if I could give him advice about the future. I gestured to my younger self to come up and tried to call him by name, but nothing came out of my mouth. Then everything took place just like I remember it as a child. My child self looked at me in terror and ran down the stairs. When I tried to follow him, I started falling down the stairs and woke up in my bed."

This was quite an amazing story. I was the only person the witness ever told it to. It is my belief he was telling the truth and not fabricating a tall tale. Did this person really make a fantastic voyage back to the past? Or was it a case of astral projection or just a dream?

CHAPTER 11

LANDS OF DREAMS AND VISIONS

There are special places throughout the world that have a reputation for being sacred and are known for their paranormal activity. In these places people often experience visions, a wide range of physiological and psychological effects, and vivid lucid dreams while spending the night. Is there really something extraordinary taking place at these locations that has a profound effect on most people, or is it nothing more than imagination and suggestion? Let's find out.

GUNGYWAMP

When many of us think of ancient mystical places, we tend to imagine a structure left over by the Druids, Greek ruins, or perhaps a lost Egyptian city. If we think about mystical places in North America, the first thing to come to mind are early Native American sites that may be several hundred to several thousand years old.

If you live in the northeastern United States, you don't have to travel to distant lands on the other side of the globe to experience a magical place, because some of the greatest mysteries in the world are right here in New England.

In Groton, Connecticut, there exists an unusual complex of carved standing stones and chambers. Called *Gungywamp*, the stone structures were built at least one thousand years before the voyage of Columbus and six hundred years before the Vikings. Many amateur archeologists who belong to the New England Antiquities Research Association (NEARA) speculate the complex may date back over two thousand years![36]

As with many ancient sites, no one knows for sure just who originally built Gungywamp or the purpose of its creation. There is some evidence that the study of astronomical alignments, the tanning of leather, and religious ceremonies were done there, but by whom?

The complex is divided into north and south sections, and one can spend the day walking through the dense woods discovering many fascinating features. These include a double circle of stones that may have been used as a grinding mill, standing stones that are carved in a conical manner that mark the trail, and a number of stone chambers.

---

36. Founded in 1964, NEARA is a nonprofit organization whose members are dedicated to, as they put it on their website, "a better understanding of our historic and prehistoric past through the study and preservation of New England's stone sites in their cultural context."

The chambers at the Gungywamp complex are different from the chambers found in the Hudson Valley. The Gungywamp chambers seem to be more recent and show very little corbelling in the construction of the walls.[37]

At the Gungywamp complex, one chamber is constructed so that during the vernal and autumnal equinoxes, sunlight streams in through an opening in the wall and illuminates a sub-chamber near the rear. Whether this was by accident or design still remains to be answered. The chamber is similar in design to the winter-solstice chamber in Kent Cliffs, New York. Here on the first day of winter during sunrise the sun's light streams through a narrow doorway and illuminates a flat stone in the rear wall.

THE CLIFF OF TEARS

At Gungywamp one can find stone mounds, cairns, walls, petroglyphs, and a rock ledge composed of pure magnetite called the "Cliff of Tears." At the Cliff of Tears visitors have been known to experience physiological and psychological reactions—which include sudden bouts of sadness, depression, and bleeding from the eyes or nails.

Gungywamp has been the focus of professional archeological explorations, which have discovered everything from arrowheads and pottery fragments to old American coins and animal bones. The exact purposes of the stone chambers are unclear, but if the site was initially a sacred complex, then it

---

37. *Corbelling* is an ancient design used in Ireland (and other places) to construct stone structures, in which rows of stones arch upward to gradually build a wall.

is possible the chambers were used in various rituals as well as for protection from the elements.

The Cliff of Tears sits on top of a massive deposit of pure iron ore in the form of magnetite. According to David Barron, who was in charge of the Gungywamp site for NEARA for many years, the Cliff of Tears got its name over twenty years ago when he was leading a group of people on a tour of the area. During an interview in 1995 with David at the Gungywamp complex, he told me:

"We had just finished most of the tour and had arrived at the Cliff of Tears when an elderly woman stepped forward who had tears flowing down her cheeks. She gave me a smile and apologetically said, 'I don't know why I'm crying. I actually feel quite happy, but here they are!' I replied, 'Don't be concerned. You are about the eighteenth person to have this happen. We don't understand the cause, but there have been folks who have experienced nosebleeds, the sudden onset of menstruation, bleeding gums, and, most of all, tears.' She was immediately relieved and said to one and all, 'Well, this must be the Cliff of Tears.' The name stuck, and since that time we have discovered that a huge vein of magnetite, reversed in polarity, extends through the cliff.[38] This has a significant effect on lowering blood pressure, causing a flow toward the extremities, fine capillaries, et cetera. I

---

38. The Cliff of Tears is the location of a negative magnetic anomaly very similar to the chambers in the Hudson Valley of New York. A negative anomaly is a sudden drop in the magnetic field of Earth. It's obvious that the magnetic force is being redirected to somewhere else. In a previous work I describe the connection between negative anomalies and dimensional portals.

suspect this is one reason why birds avoid the area, since the lodestone confuses and disorients them."

FROZEN IN TIME

I will relate to you a story told to me by a scientific researcher who had a great interest in the Gungywamp complex. This incident took place fifteen years ago, and I feel it is an important addition to my research since it is a case that involves time dilation. The individual was a geologist, scientific educator, and a graduate of Yale University. He passed away about ten years ago and was a very good friend of mine. His story appears below as he told it to me in 1993:

"I had been very interested in ancient civilizations and the possibility that the Gungywamp complex had been constructed by Bronze Age, seafaring Europeans. So, during the summer of 1991 I visited the complex with six other people, hoping to find some documentation that would satisfy my curiosity. After looking at the main complex and the chambers I noticed what I thought were etchings on a large rock near what is called the 'solstice chamber.' As I took a closer look I realized that they were not natural scratches in the rock, but it looked to me like an ancient form of Phoenician.

"I had always heard that many ancient people built sites such as this, over ground that contains a high content of energy. I was told about the Cliff of Tears and the incidents in which people who walked into that area experienced bleeding from the eyes, ears, and sometimes the nose. I had also heard stories about physiological effects, including changes in their vital signs that include pulse and blood pressure. It could be that the energy in the area is focused at the Cliff of Tears, so I had to go there to find out for myself.

"We all journeyed up the path that led to the Cliff of Tears, and as we entered I noticed a very large amount of iron ore that was scattered all over the place. Some of it looked like it had fallen down the hill in some sort of avalanche. As we got closer to the actual cliff, a few of the party members said that they felt dizzy, and I felt a little light-headed myself. At that point I heard a sound that caught my attention, and I looked away from the group. When I looked back they all looked like statues, like they were frozen. This was really bizarre, as there was no movement anywhere and not even a sound from a bird. It was as if time was standing still. This lasted about ten seconds. Then, without warning, I once again heard sounds, and the people I was with started moving and talking as if nothing had happened.

"I ran over to them and asked them if they'd noticed anything strange, but they looked at me as if *I* was strange. I told them what had just transpired, and they said according to their point of view nothing happened; everyone was moving normally. I know something very unusual had taken place. Perhaps the energy in the area actually did something to the movement of time."

It is quite possible that the energy generated at the Cliff of Tears was strong enough to cause a time dilation effect. The only explanation for this would be if our normal space was brought closer to a nearby alternate dimension or other reality. There might be a buffer or membrane between our dimension and the next. In this buffer there is no time, and as people move closer to the next adjoining dimension, someone viewing them from our normal reality may see them frozen in time. Theoretically, after crossing into the next dimension you once again enter linear time in another physical plane of existence. Since there are a great number of UFO sightings in the area, the evidence suggests that UFOs may be using the location of the chambers in New York and New England as sort of a doorway to travel back and forth from their reality to ours.

MY VISIT TO GUNGYWAMP

In 1995, fellow researcher Marianne Horrigan and I explored the Gungywamp complex. Our main task on that warm summer day was to get a better look at the Cliff of Tears. As we walked on the path that led to the iron outcrop, both of us began to feel lightheaded and then nauseous. As we got closer, we both felt as if there was a large clamp on our head and neck. Then without warning a feeling of dizziness hit us, and we had to sit down. After about ten minutes of rest, the physical symptoms stopped and we continued our journey to the front of the cliff. It was as if our bodies had to get used to the magnetic anomaly for a period of time in order for us to carry on.

I noticed three carvings on the rock, which looked like a *P* with an *X* through it. The three symbols were all in a vertical row and carved very deep in the rock, as if someone a long time ago wanted them to last through the centuries.

I recognized the symbols as being a *Chi Rho*. The Chi Rho is one of the earliest forms of the Christogram, a combination of letters forming an abbreviation for the name of Jesus Christ. The Chi Ro is formed by superimposing the first two letters in the Greek spelling of the word *Christ, chi* and *rho,* in such a way as to produce the monogram ☧. Although it is not really a cross, the Chi Rho stands for the crucifixion of Jesus as well as symbolizing his status as the Christ. Also, the Chi Ro stands for "Rabbi Christ or Christ the savior and teacher."

This was a shorthand way to write the name of Jesus Christ. It was used in the Holy Roman Empire and adopted by Irish monks in 500 AD. Could it be the Gungywamp complex was built by Irish Christians who journeyed across the Atlantic? Is it possible Gungywamp was the place where the Irish monk Saint Brendan the Navigator landed in North America almost a thousand years before Columbus? Whatever the real answer may be, Gungywamp and the Cliff of Tears are very special places where dozens of people have reported visions and otherworldly encounters.

Since my last visit I have built and acquired a number of devices that I hope will document the anomalies there. I plan to visit Gungywamp in the near future in order to carry out a detailed scientific investigation.

LAND OF DREAMS

In my files there are countless reports of people encountering all types of paranormal phenomena in places that are considered haunted or sacred in ancient and modern times. I always wondered—what would it be like to spend the night in one of these places? During sleep or relaxation the human mind is open to a great deal more than in the waking state. In the late 1990s I wanted to perform an experiment and spend the night in one of these ancient sites to see what the results might be. Doing some background research, I discovered much to my delight that author and researcher Paul Devereux had actually performed such an experiment years before, which he called *The Dragon Project*.

The Dragon Project, as the website about the project states, was founded in 1977 in order to investigate the possibility that "certain prehistoric sites had unusual forces or energies associated with them" that affected human beings in a number of ways. The Dragon Project consisted of volunteers from various disciplines who collected data at a number of sites in the United Kingdom. In the end, it was concluded that most stories about "energies" had no foundation in fact. It was the opinion of the research team that the physiological effects at the sites might be psychological in nature, produced by the subject knowing they were in a magical area.

Yet the Dragon Project did find evidence of magnetic anomalies at some sites, and inconclusive evidence of infrared and ultrasonic energy. In addition, the team of researchers found the locations that were favored by ancient megalith builders tended to have a higher than average incidence of electrical phenomena, unexplainable earthlights, and UFOs.

The Dragon Project, like most amateur studies in this area, had limited resources and decided to focus its research on the study of interaction of ancient sites with human consciousness both awake and during sleep. The dream part of this project was conducted jointly with the Saybrook Institute in San Francisco, and to the best of my knowledge the analysis is ongoing as of the writing of this book.[39]

The basic aim of the research was to conduct "dream sessions" at four selected ancient sites: at a "holy hill" in Wales and at three sites in the English county of Cornwall—a Neolithic dolmen, a Celtic holy well, and a stone chamber called a *fogou*.

The word *fogou* is the Cornish word for "cave." They are stone structures found near Iron Age settlements throughout Cornwall and in northern Scotland. The fogou consists of a buried, corbelled stone wall, tapering at the top and capped by large, flat stone slabs for a roof. Soil was heaped on top of the stone slabs to provide insulation and to keep the inner part of the chamber dry. The purpose of a fogou is unknown, and there is little evidence to suggest what they might have been used for. Archeologists speculate they might have been used for religious purposes or protection from severe storms.[40] It is doubtful they were used for food storage, since the inside is damp and most food would rot.

According to information on Paul Devereux's website (www.pauldevereux.co.uk), each of the locations selected by the project has a geophysical anomaly. The sleep volunteers

---

39. The Saybrook Institute (now Saybrook University) is an institution for humanistic studies. As the university's website states, "It is a rigorous and unique learner-centered educational institution offering advanced degrees in psychology, mind-body medicine, organizational systems, and human science."

40. *Proceedings of the Society of Antiquaries of Scotland, 1967–68*, vol. 100, 114–18.

were people of all ages, ranging from teenagers to senior citizens. Each volunteer was accompanied by a least one assistant who kept watch while the volunteer slept. When the sleeper awoke, he or she reported any dreams, which were then tape-recorded. The dream reports were sent, along with control "home" dreams from each subject, to the Saybrook Institute. The aim was to discover if the dreams the participants had at these places revealed anything extraordinary.

Do geophysical anomalies at these sites affect the dreaming mind? The Dragon Project noted that places with high background radiation "can trigger brief, vivid hallucinatory episodes in some subjects." The billion-dollar question remains unanswered, however: do ancient "magic-religious" locations where magnetic anomalies are located store information like a computer hard drive that can be downloaded by the human mind in the dream state or during mediation? Although the Dragon Project reports some interesting results, the researchers claim their findings were inconclusive.

MY RESEARCH

The fogou in the United Kingdom are very similar in size and construction to the stone chambers in the Hudson River Valley of New York. It is in New York that I conducted my own research, which was similar to the Dragon Project's.

During the mid-1990s I was doing an extensive investigation on the stone chambers in New York. With the assistance of a number of experts from different fields, we were able to establish that the stone structures were not built randomly, but rather over areas that showed a magnetic anomaly. The details and scientific findings of this research can be found in my previous works, which are listed in the bibliography at the end of this book.

Also at this time, I had no knowledge of the Dragon Project. I was very curious as to what would take place if one spent the night in or around one of the stone chambers. My question was: Are there any physical manifestations of paranormal phenomena at these locations during the night, and how would they affect the dreaming state?

The first thing to do was to find a number of volunteers who were willing to spend the night outdoors in less than ideal conditions. After inviting fifteen people to help conduct the research, only five volunteered. The number of men and women was equal, with an average age of thirty-five.

It was getting late in the year, so we planned to conduct the experiment before winter set in. We selected one site called Nimham Mountain, located in Putnam County, New York. Nimham was once Native American sacred ground, and it is named for Daniel Nimham, the last great sachem (paramount chief) of the Wappinger tribe. Since colonial days, UFOs, apparitions, and other forms of paranormal phenomena have been reported there. There is also one intact stone chamber and a number of large carved cairns, which were once standing.

We all agreed that October 26 would be a good date to spend the night. I spent the days prior to our experiment briefing the team on what we expected to accomplish, and on what to bring and how to dress.

On the 26th we all met at the base of the mountain about two hours before sunset. We planned to divide into three teams of two people each. One team would sleep in the chamber, another team in back of the chamber near the standing stones, and the final two about one hundred yards down the trail closer to the parking lot.

As night approached we made a fire, cooked hamburgers and hot dogs, and roasted marshmallows for dessert. The air was chilly and the sky was clear. I began to point out the fall constellations and the brightest stars that belong to each. To help relax the group I told the legends of the constellations from Greek and Native American mythology.

As we watched the night sky, a small sphere of light slowly moved across from north to south. It excited everyone in the group. When asked what I thought it was, my first response was it was a polar-orbiting satellite. As we watched, the light turned from white to red and flared up at least five times brighter. It was now more brilliant than the brightest stars in the sky. The object now looked like a small sphere, and it just froze in the sky directly above us. I realized at this point it was not a satellite. The object must have been very high and bright, since 10x50 binoculars offered no help in determining what it was. It was a UFO! As I watched it I thought about the many stories I'd heard from Native Americans about the spirits of the mountain.

The spirits would appear in the form of nine globes of light, all with different colors. They would then float down from the sky to the ground and take on human shape. During the twentieth century, residents who lived around the base of the mountain claim to have seen "spheres" of different-colored lights circle the mountain. With each pass the lights would get lower, as if following some type of landing pattern.

During our sighting on the mountain there was only one light. After hovering for at least two minutes, the light proceeded on its southerly course and was soon lost. Several members of the group felt it was watching us. One member of the group who is known for her psychic abilities said there were "alien beings in a ship scanning us." She felt they were going to return later that night and contact us. Was the light one of the mountain spirits or some type of other unexplainable phenomenon?

We all stayed up until midnight around a blazing fire, drinking hot chocolate. We then decided it was time to retire. Each team went to their pre-designated location and got out their sleeping bags. I and another person would be sleeping in the chamber while the other two pairs of people would spend the night at their locations in a small tent. As soon as my companion and I settled in the chamber in our sleeping bags, we both fell right to sleep.

THE NEXT MORNING

As dawn broke we all met at the chamber and packed up our gear and went out for breakfast. I asked the group not to talk about any dreams or experiences they'd had during the night until we got to my place. I could tell that each person had a story to tell by the anxious looks on their faces.

After breakfast we all went to my place to tape our experiences in order to obtain a permanent record of the previous night's experiment. Each person was to tell their own experience or dream, and I made it clear no one else could talk until it was their turn.

Everyone but me had a lucid dream that involved floating or being taken to another place by an angelic-like being or some other type of human-looking person. The places were described as having beautiful pink or blue skies with beautiful flowers that were not familiar to the person. Each person described rolling green hills with snow-capped mountains and a feeling of peace.

I, on the other hand, experienced very troubled dreams that involved family and friends. At the time I didn't know what to make of them, but the dreams later proved to be prophetic in nature, since the events portrayed in them came true within five years. But that's another story, which I don't want to cover at this time.

Also, the couple who spent the night on the lower part of the trail said a glowing ball of light came up the mountain trail and passed their tent. When it did this, they both felt dizzy, and after it passed they developed headaches in the front part of their heads, just above the eyes.

The strangest report came from the couple who pitched their tent behind the stone chamber where I was sleeping. One member of this team, a man in his forties, was a skeptic at first but changed his mind after his experience. He said at about four a.m. he heard a voice outside the tent talking in some unknown language. He was sure someone was out there, so he opened up the tent slip and looked out, but no one was there! He went back into the tent, and about ten minutes later he heard the voice again and this time saw a dark shadow move by the front of the tent. He woke his partner up, and both went out to look around but saw nothing. At first he thought it was me fooling around, but I assured him I did not leave the chamber until six a.m. My companion who stayed with me confirmed this.

It was apparent things do happen at these locations during the night, when the conscious mind is subdued and one is open to the many types of energies that flow through these places—energies considered sacred by an ancient culture.

A 2008 EXPERIMENT

There was a long lapse of time between the first attempt and the second night out at one of these sacred places. With a new group of people I wanted to try the experiment again, but this time at a place called Hawk Rock. Hawk Rock is a twenty-five-foot-tall boulder of granite that was carved by prehistoric Indians in the shape of a perched hawk. In October of 2010, the *New York Times* found Hawk Rock interesting enough to do a story on the giant megalithic carving and my research.[41]

On August 23, 2008, I, along with seven other people, spent the night at this magical place. During our stay so many incredible things took place that no one got any sleep. Things began to happen as soon as it got dark. First there was a strange human-animal sound coming from the woods;

---

43. Kevin Flynn, "A Hike into the Mystic, or Just a Walk in the Woods?" *New York Times*, October 15, 2010, C25. Online at www.nytimes.com/2010/10/15/nyregion/15hawk.html.

next, small red lights appeared in the pitch-black woods around us. They looked like tall creatures with red eyes staring at us. Finally, some type of invisible object passed over us just above the trees. As it moved slowly overhead, it distorted the tree branches and the stars in the sky. It appeared like a cubical, cloaked object. These incredible experiences are documented in my book *Files from the Edge: A Paranormal Investigator's Explorations into High Strangeness.*[42]

We are planning to spend the night once again at Hawk Rock. At that time our research team will be bringing an array of equipment that we did not have before.

HOME OF THE ANCIENT ONES

One of the most mysterious places in the southwestern United States is Chaco Canyon. It was once the home of a very ancient people called the *Anasazi*, which translates to "ancient ones" or, in some cases, "ancient enemy." UFO sightings have been reported over the ancient ruins, and visitors have claimed to hear mysterious phantom drums and to see apparitions of Indians.

Chaco Canyon is a shallow, ten-mile-long canyon located in a very remote part of what is today northwestern New Mexico. The canyon itself has been carved from ancient seabeds after centuries of erosion.

In its high-desert location over six thousand feet above sea level, Chaco is very hot in the summer and very cold in the winter. Nevertheless, evidence of a human presence in

---

44. This book was published by Llewellyn in 2010.

the area stretches back almost five thousand years. These groups were mostly nomadic until about 1,800 years ago, when farming first occurred in the area.

Then, around 850 AD, people began building in a radically different manner, with the construction of massive stone edifices that were five stories high and contained up to several hundred rooms. There were also a number of structures built to celestial alignments, especially of the sun and moon.

Construction of the city continued for three hundred years, when the area was abruptly abandoned. It's not completely clear why the people left Chaco Canyon, but theories range from alien abductions to the entire population leaving through a dimensional portal. Most archeologists believe the people of Chaco left because conditions became too harsh. They speculated many of them migrated north and became part of the Pueblo population.

When the Spanish arrived in the Southwest in the 1600s, they named the people living in New Mexico "Pueblo," the name for nineteen groups of people speaking four distinct languages. Today, modern Pueblo people claim to trace their roots to Chaco Canyon, and consider it a sacred place.

Because of its astronomical alignments, Chaco Canyon is not only of great interest to those who study ancient cultures, but also of great interest to astronomers. The most famous among these astronomical sites is the Sun Dagger, a petroglyph carved in sandstone to mark the cycles of the sun during the year.

MY VISIT TO CHACO CANYON IN 1979

Having a strong background in astronomy, the first thing I wanted to see was the Sun Dagger. It was amazing to think these ancient Native Americans were using it as a calendar to mark the beginning and end of each season. I was present during the summer solstice, on a clear day with the temperature near ninety degrees. For many years I had wanted to see this ancient petroglyph in action, and my dreams were about to come true.

At about eleven a.m. a vertical shaft of sunlight shined through an opening in the rock onto the main spiral exactly at its center. It was a spectacular sight! The park ranger told our small group that on the winter solstice, two shafts of light perfectly bracket the same spiral. Light shafts strike the center of a smaller spiral on the spring and fall equinoxes.

During my time at Chaco Canyon I had no sightings of UFOs, ghosts, or strange creatures, but I did hear several stories, from people who visited the park frequently, of phantom-like images appearing in the ruins during the day and evening. There are also legends of shapeshifting lizard beings that came from the stars. Their images can still be seen carved on the walls at Chaco.

Unfortunately, it's no longer possible to see the Sun Dagger in action. In 1989 the side of the hill eroded and shifted the large slabs of rock that now block the sun's rays. As of this writing, the Sun Dagger site is still closed to visitors.

I was very lucky to be able to see the Sun Dagger before this catastrophe took place and the area was closed to visitors. However, I often wonder why the park authorities don't restore the Sun Dagger to its former state. It seems very odd that the area was closed shorty after people in the nearby Gallo Campground reported UFOs and then black helicopters over the ruins and over the Sun Dagger location of Fajada Butte. Once again we see that strange phenomena and possible government involvement are prominent in areas that are considered sacred ground.

CHAPTER 12

THE UNSEEN UNIVERSE

After reading my books, the reader may think real paranormal cases are common, but the truth is they are not. I only published the cases about which I was positive something unexplainable took place. If one takes the total number of cases I have looked into and compares this number with those that were unexplained, the percentage is very low.

Although my field investigations have slowed down considerably since I began this research over three decades ago, the caseload has not diminished. I have personally investigated over a thousand claims of encounters with the paranormal. As a result of this research I am convinced there are other realms of existence, creatures, and forces with which we are not familiar and that are not part of our everyday reality. I believe there is an unseen world that exists all around us. We only are able to perceive a very small part of the cosmos, and what we cannot see or detect with our technology may be a very large portion of the total universe.

Our reality is based on the interaction our senses have with subatomic particles. What we call energy is actually a flow of elementary particles that are photonic in nature. These particles are composed of two-dimensional strings that vibrate at a particular frequency. The vibration of the string will determine what type of particle is formed.

When electrons are bombarded by other elementary particles, they vibrate and radiate photons. The frequency or energy level of the photons will depend on how fast the strings that make up electrons vibrate. This includes visible light, which is composed of those photonic particles that allow humans to experience vision. This sense can be misleading in determining what is real and what is not. The photons that transmit through the human eye only carry images of reality, and our brains are left to interpret the sometimes jumbled collection of information. Sometimes this photonic information is only partially received, and on occasion the object is not physically there. When this takes place, our concept of reality is greatly altered.

There are still many forces that are a mystery to us. For example, where does the energy that vibrates the strings come from? This energy would not be composed of particles, but of true energy. It is possible this energy that is used to create what we call a physical reality actually emits from another universe.

The idea that our universe is formed and bound together by invisible bonds of energy was not imagined by *Star Wars* creator George Lucas. The Divine Force, as it was called in the fourteenth century, was proposed by the mystics of that day. They believed this force originated from the creator of the universe and flowed through all things in our reality. This unseen energy that powers our realism has also been known by the ancient Chinese and called *chi*.

This notion of another realm of pure energy leads to many possibilities. Our reality could be changed slowly or very quickly depending upon how much or little the strings that make up our physical universe vibrate. This is something incredible to think about; perhaps we do really exist in a Matrix controlled by the creator of the universe or a host of advanced beings.

This could also mean the human physical body is only a small part of our real form. Recently, while visiting the Chuang Yen Monastery in New York, I came across a large blackboard outside the main Buddha hall that had messages on it written by monks, nuns, masters, and people who come there to study. One written message caught my attention. It simply said, "You are not a body with a soul, but a soul with a body."

DARK ENERGY

Perhaps the pure energy with which the human soul is composed also vibrates the strings that create particles that make up your physical body. Theoretical physicists believe this as-yet undetectable energy is real, since they can see its secondary effect on matter in our universe. It has been mistakenly called *dark energy* since its effects can be measured, but this elusive force cannot be seen with our instruments.

In the 1990s two teams of astronomers, one at the Lawrence Berkeley National Laboratory and the other the High-Z Supernova Search Team, were looking for distant supernovae in order to measure the expansion rate of the universe. They expected to find that the expansion of the universe was slowing down. Instead, the scientists found something totally unexpected—they discovered the expansion of the universe was accelerating!

Since there is not enough matter in the universe to cause the observed accelerated expansion, a dark energy or force was proposed. This idea of dark energy could be the power source causing acceleration and expansion of the physical universe and the origin of all matter.

Dark energy remains a complete mystery. The term *dark energy* simply refers to some kind of invisible "stuff" that must fill the vast reaches of empty space in the universe in order to be able to make space accelerate while it is expanding. In this sense, it is a "field," just like an electric or a magnetic field, both of which are produced by electromagnetic energy from vibrating electrons.

But this analogy can only be taken so far, because we can readily observe electromagnetic energy via the particle that carries it, the photon. Could it be that dark energy is not photonic in nature and emits from another reality? Could it be the power source that drives our universe?

Some astronomers identify dark energy with Albert Einstein's cosmological constant. Einstein introduced this constant into his general theory of relativity when he saw that his model was predicting an expanding universe, which was contrary to the evidence for a static universe that he and other physicists had in the early twentieth century. With Edwin Hubble's discovery of the expansion of the universe, Einstein dismissed his constant.

When compared to the theory of dark energy, Einstein's cosmological constant acts like a reservoir that stores energy. This reservoir of energy would increase as the universe expands, much like pouring more water into a larger and larger container. If this is so, the dark energy that continues to fill the void as the galaxies expand must be coming from somewhere. This theoretical model supports the concept of a multidimensional universe.

The theory of "dark energy" also indicates the existence of another universe, one composed of pure energy in which our reality is only a reflection. Perhaps this other place is the real universe, and our world is nothing more than a manifestation of it.

I have heard several stories from Buddhist monks and other people looking for enlightenment who claim that once you are able to transcend physical consciousness, this other reality can be viewed. During periods of deep meditation, these people have reported encounters with other beings and forces that are not part of our physical reality. Perhaps when ordinary human beings get a glimpse of these other realities, they don't understand what they are experiencing. As a result of fear and lack of understanding, they call the experience "supernatural" or "paranormal."

I really have no answers to any of the mysteries presented in this book. I do believe we are a small part of a much bigger existence that transcends the perceptions of our five senses.

There are many more case studies and investigations in my files that are still not published. Many of these cases involve encounters with phantom-like beings and extraordinary people who seem to have the ability to heal and help the sick get well by a simple touch. Perhaps I will publish these cases in the near future. To me they represent more evidence of this unseen reality to which we are connected on many levels.

In closing, we have to consider that the paranormal is not really outside normal reality; it is all part of a complex universe that we share with a multitude of other beings and forces.

FURTHER READING

Other than the books mentioned below, I suggest that the reader obtain my previous books to get a full understanding of how my work into the paranormal evolved over the years.

Barnett, Charles, and Phil Miller. *The Battle of the Alamo*. Bloomington, MN: Capstone Press, 2005.

Beckley, Timothy Green, and Sean Casteel. *Round Trip to Hell in a Flying Saucer*. New Brunswick, NJ: Global Communications, 2011.

Devereux, Paul. *Earth Lights Revelation*. London: Blandford Press, 1989.

Dudley, Gary P. *The Legend of Dudleytown: Solving Legends through Genealogical and Historical Research*. Westminster, MD: Heritage Books, Inc., 2001. (The best source of information on Dudleyville. Interestingly enough, the author is the Reverend Gary P. Dudley.)

Goforth, August, and Timothy Gray. *The Risen*. New York: Teapot Books, 2009.

Guiley, Rosemary Ellen. *The Encyclopedia of Demons & Demonology*. New York: Checkmark Books, 2009.

———. *The Encyclopedia of Ghosts and Spirits*, 3rd ed. New York: Facts on File, 2007.

Hynek, J. Allen. *The UFO Experience*. New York: Ballantine, 1974.

Joseph, Frank. *Unearthing Ancient America*. Franklin Lakes, NJ: Career Press, 2009.

Kelleher, Colm, and George Knapp. *Hunt for the Skinwalker*. New York: Paraview Books, 2005.

Levy, Joel. *Fabulous Creatures and Other Magical Beings*. London: Carroll and Brown, 2007.

Nelson, Robert A. "Marian Apparitions & Prophecies," 2000. Online at www.rexresearch.com/mary/maryapps .htm. (For information on Marian manifestations, this is one of the most informative webpages.)

Skinner, Charles M. *Myths & Legends of Our Own Land*. Philadelphia: J. B. Lippincott, 1896.

BIBLIOGRAPHY

The majority of the information used for this book was obtained from my files and previously published works. However, the following resources were used to check on facts and update data.

Barry, J. D. *Ball Lightning and Bead Lightning; Extreme Forms of Atmospheric Electricity*. New York: Plenum Press, 1980.

Brooks, Marla. *Ghosts of Hollywood: The Show Still Goes On*. Atglen, PA: Schiffer Publishing, 2008.

"Chaco Culture National Historical Park." U.S. National Park Service, http://www.nps.gov/chcu/index.htm. Accessed June 22, 2010.

Clifton, Timothy. "Does Dark Energy Really Exist?" *Scientific American*, volume 300, pp. 47–55, April 2009.

Coleman, Peter. *Great Balls of Fire: A Unified Theory of Ball Lightning, UFOs*. Christchurch, New Zealand: Foreshine Press, 2004.

Delany, Patrick. *History of New Haven Colony*. New Haven, CT: Yale University Press, 1926.

DeLuca, Dan W., and Dione Longley. *The Old Leather Man: Historical Accounts of a Connecticut Legend*. Middletown, CT: Wesleyan University Press, 2008.

Devereux, Paul. *Secrets of Ancient and Sacred Places: The World's Mysterious Heritage*. London: Blanford Press, 1996.

Fell, Barry. *American BC Ancient Settlers in the New World*. New York: Pocket Books, 1989.

Gore, Ellard. *Astronomical Observations and Theories of Sir William Herschel*. Whitefish, MT: Erwood-Kessinger Publishing, 1981.

Grosvenor, Lemuel. *The Life and Character of Major General Putnam*; from an address delivered in 1885 at a meeting in Redding, Connecticut.

Guiley, Rosemary Ellen, and Philip J. Imbrogno. *The Vengeful Djinn: Unveiling the Hidden Agenda of Genies*. Woodbury, MN: Llewellyn, 2011. (Also see www.djinnuniverse .com/)

Hawking, Stephen. *The Universe in Short*. New York: Bantam, 2001.

Hoffer, Peter. *The Salem Witchcraft Trials: A Legal History*. Lawrence, KS: University of Kansas Press, 1997.

Imbrogno, Philip J. *Files from the Edge: A Paranormal Investigator's Explorations into High Strangeness*. Woodbury, MN: Llewellyn, 2010.

———. *Interdimensional Universe: The New Science of UFOs, Paranormal Phenomena & Otherdimensional Beings*. Woodbury, MN: Llewellyn, 2008.

———. *Ultraterrestrial Contact: A Paranormal Investigator's Explorations into the Hidden Abduction Epidemic*. Woodbury, MN: Llewellyn, 2010.

Imbrogno, Philip J., and Marianne Horrigan. *Celtic Mysteries: Windows to Another Dimension in America's Northeast*. New York: Cosimo Publishing, 2005.

Imbrogno, Philip J., J. Allen Hynek, and Bob Pratt. *Night Siege: The Hudson Valley UFO Sightings*. St. Paul, MN: Llewellyn, 1998.

International 7th International Symposium on Ball Lightning, St. Louis Missouri (http://www.umsl.edu/~handelp/BLConference.html). Accessed May 24, 2010.

Irving, Washington. *The Legend of Sleepy Hollow*. New York: Tor-Boks Books, reprinted 1991.

Joslin, Benjamin. *Observations on Solar and Lunar Columns, Halos, the Aurora Borealis, and Auroral Clouds, and Remarks on the Connection between These Phenomena and Crystals*. New York: University of the State of New York, 1836.

Keel, John A. *The Complete Guide to Mysterious Beings*. New York: Tor Books, 2002.

Martin, John. *Roses, Fountains, and Gold: The Virgin Mary in History, Art, and Apparition*. San Francisco: Ignatius Press, 1998.

May, Jo. *Fogou: Gateway to the Underworld*. Glastonbury, UK: Gothic Image Publications, 1996.

Myers, John. *The Alamo*. Charlotte, NC: Bison Publishing, 1973.

New England Antiquities Research Association (NEARA). http://www. neara.org. Accessed October 12, 2010.

Owlsbury-Duddleyville. Various documents at Cornwall, Connecticut Historical Society.

Powlett, Catherine Lucy Wilhelmina. *The True Story of Kaspar Hauser, from Official Documents*. London: Macmillan, 1893.

Public Record Archives. Land Deeds and Contracts in Greenwich, 1740–1910, Town Hall, Greenwich, CT.

Putnam County Archives and Records. Putnam County, New York. Documents concerning land deeds and news clippings from 1810–1949.

Taylor James T. *The History of Tarrytown, New York*. White Plains, NY: The County of Westchester, 1937.

Tomlinson, Richard G. *Witchcraft Trials of Connecticut*. Hartford, CT: Research, Inc., 1978.

Various authors. *A History of American Indians in the State of Connecticut*. Historical document dated 1879. Native American section. The Bruce Museum, Greenwich, CT.

Various unknown authors. Historical documents of Redding Park. Redding, Connecticut 1780–1921. Documents found at Redding Park Museum. Accessed June 12, 2009.

Walsh, William Thomas. *Our Lady of Fátima*. Memphis, TN: Image Books, 1954.

INDEX

A

Alamo, 161–176
Aykroyd, Dan, 177

B

Baddock, Frederick,
    48
Balanced Rock, 7–8
ball lightning, 61–63
Bayside, New York, 125–
    128, 130, 139
Bethel, Connecticut, 40,
    95–96
Brendan (saint), 222
Brophy, John, 181–182

C

Celtic explorers, 9
Chaco Canyon, 231–233
Chi Ro, 222
Clark, William,
    182
Cliff of Tears, 217–222
Columbus, Christopher,
    8–9, 216, 222
Coptic Church, 119
Corona Park, New York,
    139
Crane, Ichabod, 68–69
Crockett, Davy, 163,
    169–170, 176

D

Danbury, Connecticut, 40, 105, 148, 185, 202
dark energy, 25, 55, 100, 237–239
"Dark Entrance," 182
Denolda, John, 48
Devereux, Paul, 223–224
Devil's Hopyard, 155, 157–160
djinn, 140–141, 143, 166, 199, 204
dolmen, 7–9, 224
Dragon Project, 223, 225–226
Druids, 9, 52, 215
Dudley, Edmund, 177–183, 185–189
Dudleyville, Connecticut, 177–183, 185–189

E

Einstein, Albert, 238–239
electronic voice phenomena (EVP), 65–66, 78, 159, 204
Environmental Protection Agency (EPA), 62
Exodus, 81–82

F

Fairfield, Connecticut, 88, 92, 93, 95–96, 202
Fátima, Portugal, 115, 117–118, 129
Files from the Edge (book), xiv, 195, 231
fogou, 224–225

G

Gallows Hill (Redding, Connecticut), 148, 152–153
glacial erratic, 7–8
Gold, Samuel, 147
grandfather paradox, 192–193
Green Witch, 81, 87–88, 95–99, 101–102, 104–105
Greenwich, Connecticut, 96
Groundhog Day (film), 193
Gungywamp, 215–219, 221–222

H

Hartford, Connecticut, 27, 82, 84, 86–87, 92, 95, 186, 202
Hauser, Kaspar, 198–200
Hawk Rock, 230–231

Heidenhall, Marcus, 49

Hollister, Gerson, 180

Holzer, Hans, xii–xiii

Hubble, Edwin, 239

Hudson Valley, New York, 46, 67, 74, 183, 195–196, 201, 217–218, 225

Hynek, J. Allen, xiv, xviii, 6, 174

I

Interdimensional Universe (book), 78, 185, 195

K

Kent Cliffs, New York, 217

Knapp, Goodwife, 87–94, 96–98, 103

Knapp, Roger, 87–94, 96–98, 103

L

La Salette, France, 113

Labouré, Catherine, 113

Leatherman, 201–205

Legend of Sleepy Hollow, The, 65–69, 78–79, 100–101

Louten, George and Klara, 28, 29, 31–32, 34

Lucas, George, 237

Lueken, Veronica, 127

M

Mattabesic Indians, 26

Medjugorje, Bosnia and Herzegovina, 120, 123–124

Men in Black (film), 125, 196

men in black (MIB), 197–198, 209

Merwin, Jesse, 69

Mohegan Indians, 26

Munsee Indians, 26–27, 29

Murray, Bill, 193

N

New England Antiquities Research Organization (NEARA), 216, 218

New Haven Colony, 89–92, 95, 99

New York Times, 52, 59, 82, 126, 230

Niantic Indians, 26

Night Siege (book), 46, 74

Nimham Mountain, 226
North Salem, New York,
    7–8, 202

O
Old Dutch cemetery, 70–75,
    77
Our Lady of Fátima, 115,
    117–118, 129
Owlsbury. *See* Dudleyville,
    Connecticut

P
paranormal filing system,
    xx–xxii
Pequot Indians, 26
Phillips' Cave, 153–155
photons, 236, 238
Putnam County, New York,
    46–47, 52, 62–63, 82,
    204, 226
Putnam Park, 145–150,
    152–155
Putnam, Israel, 145, 147, 154

Q
Queens, New York, 125–
    126, 128, 130, 136,
    138

R
Redding, Connecticut,
    95–96, 98–99, 145, 147,
    153–154
Rip Van Winkle, 67

S
Salem, Massachusetts, 7–8,
    83, 85–86, 177, 202
San Antonio, Texas,
    161–162, 166–167, 170,
    175–176
Shepard, Odell, 154–155
Sleepy Hollow, New York,
    65–69, 71–73, 75–76,
    79–80, 101, 177, 203
Soubirous, Bernadette, 114
Sun Dagger, 232–234
Sunnyside (estate), 78, 80

T
Tanner, William, 180
transient lunar phenomena
    (TLP), 4–5

U
UFOs, xii, xiv, xvii, xix–xx,
    xxiii, 4–7, 22, 46, 49,
    67, 74, 78, 95, 125–126,

131–132, 138, 140, 149,
174–175, 195–198, 204,
208, 221, 223, 226–227,
231, 233–234

Underground Railroad, 15

V

Van Tassel, Katrina, 69

Virgin Mary, 107, 112–115,
117–119, 121, 123–126,

128–130, 132–133, 135,
138

W

will o' the wisp, 49–50

Woodward, Walter, 84

Z

Zaffis, John, 38

TO WRITE TO THE AUTHOR

If you wish to contact the author or would like more information about this book, please write to the author in care of Llewellyn Worldwide Ltd. and we will forward your request. Both the author and publisher appreciate hearing from you and learning of your enjoyment of this book and how it has helped you. Llewellyn Worldwide Ltd. cannot guarantee that every letter written to the author can be answered, but all will be forwarded. Please write to:

Philip J. Imbrogno
C/o Llewellyn Worldwide
2143 Wooddale Drive
Woodbury, MN 55125-2989

Please enclose a self-addressed stamped envelope for reply,
or $1.00 to cover costs. If outside the USA, enclose
an international postal reply coupon.

Many of Llewellyn's authors have websites with additional information and resources. For more information, please visit our website at http://www.llewellyn.com.

FILES
FROM THE
EDGE

A PARANORMAL
INVESTIGATOR'S
EXPLORATIONS
INTO HIGH
STRANGENESS

PHILIP J. IMBROGNO

Files From the Edge

A Paranormal Investigator's Explorations into High Strangeness

PHILIP J. IMBROGNO

Ghost lights, otherworldly creatures, visits from another dimension—the most bizarre and amazing case studies from a renowned paranormal investigator are presented here.

In this thirty-year career, Philip J. Imbrogno has researched a vast array of fascinating supernatural phenomena—the perpetually haunted mines of Putnam County, New York; encounters with strange entities at sacred megalithic stones; Bigfoot, yeti, and other humanoids; sea creatures; psychic phenomena; the dangerous jinn; and a vast array of life forms from other worlds. The author's objective, scientific analysis—combined with credible witness testimonials and Imbrogno's own thrilling experiences—provides eye-opening, convincing evidence of our multidimensional universe.

978-0-7387-1881-1, 336 pp., 5 $^3/_{16}$ x 8   **$17.95**

ULTRATERRESTRIAL CONTACT

A PARANORMAL
INVESTIGATOR'S
EXPLORATIONS
INTO THE HIDDEN
ABDUCTION EPIDEMIC

PHILIP J. IMBROGNO

Ultraterrestrial Contact

A Paranormal Investigator's Explorations into the Hidden Abduction Epidemic

PHILIP J. IMBROGNO

This book investigates the most extreme and bizarre UFO reports—cases that most UFO investigators are afraid to tackle—and presents a radical new quantum approach to understanding the contact phenomenon.

When Philip Imbrogno collaborated with famed UFO researcher Dr. J. Allen Hynek on their book *Night Siege*, Dr. Hynek requested that the more sensational cases of "high strangeness"—claims of contact with not only alien intelligence, but also angels, demons, and otherdimensional beings—remain unpublished. Hynek thought the reports would detract from the credibility of the entire ET investigation field. *Ultraterrestrial Contact* reveals the details of these controversial reports for the first time and presents Imbrogno's startling scientific conclusions from thirty years of research into the alien contact phenomenon.

978-0-7387-1959-7, 336 pp., 5 ³/₁₆ x 8   **$17.95**

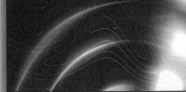

PHILIP IMBROGNO

INTERDIMENSIONAL
UNIVERSE

THE NEW SCIENCE OF UFOS,
PARANORMAL PHENOMENA
& OTHERDIMENSIONAL BEINGS

Interdimensional Universe
The New Science of UFOs, Paranormal Phenomena & Otherdimensional Beings

PHILIP IMBROGNO

Over the course of his decades of investigation into UFOs—including his own field research, photographic evidence, and meticulously compiled case studies—Philip Imbrogno has provided fascinating new insight into paranormal phenomena. In this book, he reveals for the first time the detailed experiences of prominent paranormal experts as well as his own firsthand experiences. Using the latest quantum theories, Imbrogno sheds new light on classic UFO cases, government cover-ups, and the hidden connections between UFOs and other unexplained phenomena—from crop circles and animal mutilations to angels and jinn (or genies).

Imbrogno's intimate knowledge includes the very early UFO activities as well as present-day sightings. He personally investigated four of the best-known UFO flaps of the modern era—Hudson Valley, Phoenix lights, the Belgium sightings, and the Gulf Breeze sightings—and shares information never released before, including photographic evidence that something very unusual is taking place on planet Earth.

978-0-7387-1347-2, 312 pp., 5 $^{3}/_{16}$ x 8   **$17.95**
